INTRODUCTIO

The West Midlands county is home to an extraordinary number of places to see and activities to enjoy. From world class museums and record-breaking theatres to national nature reserves and award-winning gardens, no matter the weather this comprehensive guide will provide all the inspiration you need for a day out to remember!

The West Midlands county consists of seven metropolitan boroughs: the City of **Birmingham**, the City of **Coventry** and the City of **Wolverhampton**, as well as the boroughs of **Dudley**, **Sandwell**, **Solihull** and Walsall. Use the index or the colour coding in this book to find great places to visit in each location.

The you'll see throughout the book, whether you're looking for a free day out, a fully accessible venue or the perfect place to visit with kids, you'll have all the information you need at your fingertips. Every listing has a website address too so you can find up to date opening days and times with ease. We recommend checking each venues website prior to arranging a visit to ensure you have the latest information.

Wherever you decide to visit we know you'll enjoy discovering this welcoming county full of eclectic attractions and unique experiences...

 Free admission

 Paid admission

 Free Admission – *Some activities or exhibitions may charge*

 Family friendly

 Wheelchair accessible

 Lift access

 Accessible toilets

 Steps/uneven terrain

 Induction loops

 Audio description

 Subtitles

 Service dogs only

 Virtual tour

 Baby changing facilities

 Dog friendly areas - *check venue website for details*

CONTENTS

BIRMINGHAM

St Philips Cathedral / ©Birmingham Cathedral

Aston Hall | ©Birmingham Museums Trust

ASTON HALL

Birmingham Museums Trust
Trinity Road, Aston, B6 6JD

Explore the splendour of one of the last great houses built in the Jacobean style. Aston Hall is a magnificent 17th-century red-brick mansion situated in the picturesque Aston Park on the north side of Birmingham. Steeped in history, and restored to its former Jacobean splendour, Aston Hall is now a Grade I Listed building, and is hugely popular with visitors of all ages.

🌐 birminghammuseums.org.uk/aston
✉ hello@birminghammuseums.org.uk

The Barber Institute / ©John Jones

THE BARBER INSTITUTE OF FINE ARTS

University of Birmingham
University of Birmingham, Edgbaston, B15 2TS

Masterpieces by many of the greatest names in Western art – including Botticelli, Rubens, Turner, Gainsborough, Rossetti, Monet, Renoir, Rodin, Degas, Gauguin and Van Gogh – grace the galleries in the Barber's Grade I Listed Art Deco building. Founded in 1932 by Hattie, Lady Barber, in memory of her husband, the Barber is also home to one of Europe's most important coin collections, and hosts an exciting programme of temporary exhibitions, concerts by internationally recognised classical musicians, plus gallery talks, workshops and family activities.

🌐 barber.org.uk/welcome
✉ info@barber.org.uk

Aston Hall | ©Birmingham Museums Trust / Verity E Milligan

THE BIRMINGHAM CONTEMPORARY ART GALLERY

Unit 5 Utilita Arena, King Edward's Road, B1 2AA

Located a short walk from Brindleyplace overlooking the canal, the Birmingham Contemporary Art Gallery is the first hybrid art gallery in the Midlands, showcasing some of the region's finest emerging and established artists, while using the gallery space in unconventional ways to engage the public. The gallery is involved in running creative community initiatives that connect local communities while promoting shared cultural heritages and inclusion through art, with the aim being to use the arts to promote social engagement and to encourage young artists to share in and occupy the creative space.

🌐 birmingham-cag.uk

✉ info@birmingham-cag.uk

BIRMINGHAM MUSEUM & ART GALLERY

Birmingham Museums Trust

Chamberlain Square, Birmingham, B3 3DH

Housed in a landmark Grade II° Listed building, Birmingham Museum & Art Gallery is a world class museum in the heart of the city, that reflects the best of Birmingham to the world, and the world to Birmingham. First opened in 1885, there are over 40 galleries to explore displaying art, social history, archaeology and ethnography, along with the famous Staffordshire Hoard. In addition to the permanent galleries, there is a diverse exhibition programme that offers a series of changing exhibitions throughout the year and a wide range of family friendly activities for all ages. During your visit why not treat yourself to lunch or even afternoon tea in the award-winning Edwardian Tea Rooms, where you can experience Birmingham's only 'press for Champagne' service?

🌐 birminghammuseums.org.uk/bmag

✉ hello@birminghammuseums.org.uk

Blakesley Hall / ©Birmingham Museums Trust

Blakesley Hall / ©Birmingham Museums Trust / Verity E Milligan

BLAKESLEY HALL

Birmingham Museums Trust
Blakesley Road, Yardley, B25 8RN

Discover a fine Tudor house and beautiful gardens just a few miles from the heart of the city. Blakesley Hall is a timber-framed house built in 1590 by Richard Smalbroke, a member of one of Birmingham's leading merchant families. More than 400 years later, beautiful Blakesley is still a haven, secluded from the avenues of modern houses that lie beyond its gates. The house is furnished using an inventory taken in the 17th-century and reflects the lifestyle of a wealthy family of the late Tudor and Stuart periods of English history.

🌐 birminghammuseums.org.uk/blakesley
✉ hello@birminghammuseums.org.uk

THE COFFIN WORKS

13-15 Fleet Street, Jewellery Quarter, B3 1JP

The shelves and workbenches at the Coffin Works are full of original stock and tools of the trade. With the original machinery working again, you can truly experience how this old Jewellery Quarter firm once operated on a day-to-day basis, producing some of the worlds finest coffin furniture, including the fittings for the funerals of Joseph Chamberlain, Winston Churchill and the Queen Mother. Situated in the Jewellery Quarter Conservation Area, the Coffin Works museum educates visitors about the social and industrial history of the site, which operated from 1894–1998 as a coffin furniture factory.

🌐 coffinworks.org
✉ newmanbrothers@coffinworks.org

The Coffin Works / ©Luke Unsworth

Eastside projects / ©Sonia Boyce

EASTSIDE PROJECTS

86 Heath Mill Lane, Digbeth, B9 4AR

Aiming to make art public, Eastside Projects runs a large evolving gallery space in Digbeth which is free, and is imagined and organised by artists. Eastside Projects calls itself an artist run multiverse – commissioning, producing and exhibiting experimental art practices and demonstrate ways in which art may be useful as part of society. Join the Extra Ordinary People artists programme, stream artworks online or visit the unusual building full of short and long term artworks.

🌐 eastsideprojects.org

✉ info@eastsideprojects.org

GRAND UNION – MINERVA WORKS DIGBETH

19 Minerva Works, Fazeley Street, Digbeth, B5 5RS

Grand Union is a gallery and artists' studios complex situated in Digbeth, with the aim of bringing the public closer to art and artists. It hosts a free programme of public exhibitions and events, with many opportunities to share food and ideas. Creating numerous contexts

for art and life to intersect, its work places an emphasis on the importance of collaboration and artistic research. Many of these projects take place outside of the gallery, across the city and the gallery also provides frequent opportunities for members of the public to visit behind the scenes.

🌐 grand-union.org.uk

✉ info@grand-union.org.uk

IKON GALLERY

1 Oozells Square, Brindleyplace, B1 2HS

Housed in a magnificent Victorian school building, the Ikon Gallery is an internationally acclaimed contemporary art venue. The gallery features temporary exhibitions over two floors, and shows work by artists from around the world in a variety of media including sound, film, mixed media, photography, painting, sculpture and installation. Visitors can also visit the cafe and bookshop.

🌐 ikon-gallery.org

Ikon Gallery / ©Ikon Gallery

Lapworth Museum of Geology / ©Greg Milner

LAPWORTH MUSEUM OF GEOLOGY
University of Birmingham
School of Geography, Earth and Environmental Sciences, University of Birmingham, Edgbaston, B15 2TT

The Lapworth Museum of Geology holds the finest and most extensive collections of fossils, minerals and rocks in the Midlands. Dating back to 1880, it is one of the oldest specialist geological museums in the UK with state-of-the-art galleries and a range of innovative and interactive exhibits. The Lapworth Museum showcases exceptional objects from one of the UK's most outstanding geological collections. From rocks and fossils to volcanoes, earthquakes, and even dinosaurs, the Museum captures the imagination of all ages.

🌐 lapworth.bham.ac.uk
✉ lapworth@contacts.bham.ac.uk

Museum of the Jewellery Quarter / ©Birmingham Museums Trust / Verity E Milligan

MUSEUM COLLECTION CENTRE

Birmingham Museums Trust
25 Dollman Street, Nechells, B7 4RQ

One of the UK's largest museum stores, the Museum Collection Centre is a 1.5 hectare site that holds 80 per cent of Birmingham Museums' stored collections under one roof. Among the thousands of objects, there are steam engines, sculptures, an entire collection of Austin, Rover and MG motor cars and even a red phone box.

🌐 birminghammuseums.org.uk/collection/
    museum-collection-centre

✉ hello@birminghammuseums.org.uk

MUSEUM OF THE JEWELLERY QUARTER

Birmingham Museums Trust
75-80 Vyse Street, Jewellery Quarter, B18 6HA

Built around a perfectly preserved jewellery workshop, the Museum of the Jewellery Quarter offers a unique glimpse of working life in Birmingham's famous Jewellery Quarter. When the proprietors of the Smith & Pepper jewellery manufacturing firm retired in 1981, they simply ceased trading and locked the door, unaware they would be leaving a time capsule for future generations. Today the factory is a remarkable museum, which tells the story of the Jewellery Quarter and Birmingham's renowned jewellery and metalworking heritage.

🌐 birminghammuseums.org.uk/jewellery

✉ hello@birminghammuseums.org.uk

The Pen Museum / ©The Pen Museum

THE PEN MUSEUM
The Argent Centre, 60 Frederick Street,
Jewellery Quarter, B1 3HS

The Pen Museum is the only museum in the UK dedicated to preserving and celebrating Birmingham's important role in developing the steel pen trade during the 19th-century. At the peak of production an estimated 8,000 workers, of which 70 per cent were women, were employed in the pen trade and the Pen Museum explores how the mass production of affordable pens helped improve literacy on a worldwide basis. Birmingham's pen trade development and heritage is showcased via exhibition displays, demonstrations, and activities that narrate the important legacy of skilled pen workers, influential entrepreneurs and prominent manufacturers.

🌐 penmuseum.org.uk
✉ enquiries@penmuseum.org.uk

Sarehole Mill / ©Birmingham Museums Trust

RBSA GALLERY

Royal Birmingham Society of Artists
4 Brook Street, Jewellery Quarter, B3 1SA

Situated in the historic Jewellery Quarter, a short walk from the city centre, the RBSA Gallery is an artist-led charity which supports artists and promotes engagement with the visual arts through a range of exhibitions, events and workshops. Owned by the Royal Birmingham Society of Artists, it is one of a few galleries to be owned by and run for artists. It has a changing programme of exhibitions on two floors, ground floor cafe and craft wall spaces. The ground floor also houses the craft gallery, which has established a reputation as the place to find exciting and unique handmade jewellery.

🌐 rbsa.org.uk
✉ rbsagallery@rbsa.org.uk

SAREHOLE MILL

Birmingham Museums Trust
Cole Bank Road, Birmingham, B13 0BD

Famous for its association with author JRR Tolkien, this 250 year old watermill is a must visit for Tolkienites and history lovers alike. There has been a mill on the site since 1542, with the current building dating from the mid-18th-century. In the 1850s a steam engine was installed, and a chimney built, which provides Sarehole Mill with its distinctive silhouette. The mill also has connections with industrialist Matthew Boulton, who leased the mill between 1756 and 1761 and used it as a 'flatting mill', producing sheet metal used for button manufacturing. Sarehole Mill is now home to a modern-day bakery which serves delicious freshly baked treats! You can enjoy a pizza in the courtyard, or pre-order a freshly baked loaf of bread with a Bake and Take service available at the community shop.

🌐 birminghammuseums.org.uk/sarehole
✉ hello@birminghammuseums.org.uk

Selly Manor Museum / ©Selly Manor Museum & Bournville Village Trust

SELLY MANOR MUSEUM

Bournville Village Trust
Maple Road, Bournville, B30 2AE

Situated in the heart of Bournville, the Selly Manor Museum has a fascinating history to discover. Selly Manor is a timber-framed building, moved to its current location in 1916 by chocolate manufacturer and philanthropist George Cadbury. The museum's two distinct and beautiful buildings have fascinating histories, with close links to the world famous chocolate-maker and his son Laurence who are responsible for much of the fantastic collection. There are opportunities for kids play, dressing up, objects to handle and armour to try on.

🌐 sellymanormuseum.org.uk
✉ sellymanor@bvt.org.uk

Soho House / ©Birmingham Museums Trust / Verity E Milligan

SOHO HOUSE

Birmingham Museums Trust
Soho Avenue, Handsworth, B18 5LB

The elegant Georgian home of the industrialist and entrepreneur Matthew Boulton from 1766 to 1809, Soho House has been beautifully restored and reflects the fashions and tastes of the late Georgian period. There is also the chance to see some of the products of Boulton's nearby factory – where buttons and buckles, clocks and vases, silver and Sheffield plate tableware were made – and where he developed the steam engine in partnership with James Watt.

🌐 birminghammuseums.org.uk/soho
✉ hello@birminghammuseums.org.uk

THINKTANK

Birmingham Museums Trust
Millennium Point, Curzon Street,
Birmingham, B4 7XG

Thinktank, Birmingham's award-winning science museum, offers an enlightening and fun-packed day out for the family. From steam engines and talking robots through to gurgling guts and a chocolate wrapping machine, Thinktank has over 200 displays exploring science and technology. Housed inside the impressive Millennium Point building, at Thinktank you will find four floors of hands-on exhibits and historical collections that will amaze and inspire you, showing you the science of the world all around us. Explore MiniBrum, an interactive gallery where under 8s can be in charge in their very own city. There is also a 4K planetarium, science garden, plus an exciting programme of events and activities.

🌐 birminghammuseums.org.uk/thinktank
✉ hello@birminghammuseums.org.uk

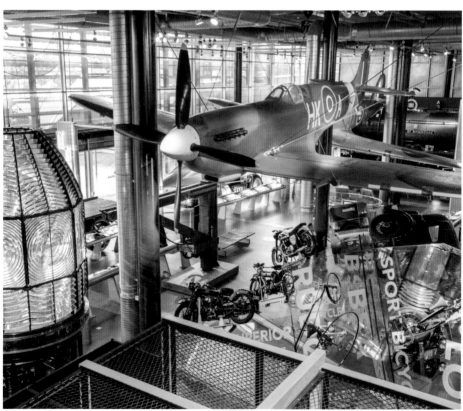

Thinktank / ©Birmingham Museums Trust

Winterbourne House and Garden / ©Greg Milner

Weoley Castle / ©Birmingham Museums Trust

WEOLEY CASTLE

Birmingham Museums Trust
Alwold Road, Northfield, B29 5RJ

The ruins of Weoley Castle are over 750 years old and are the remains of an impressive fortified manor house, built as a hunting lodge by the Lords of Dudley complete with moat, towers, battlements and arrow slits. The castle once stood within 1,000 acres of deer park which extended almost as far as the city centre. The ruins are one of the oldest buildings still visible in Birmingham and are classified as a Scheduled Ancient Monument of national importance. The site is host to a variety of family activities and events throughout the year, and visitors can view the site from the fully accessible viewing platform.

🌐 birminghammuseums.org.uk/weoley

✉ hello@birminghammuseums.org.uk

WINTERBOURNE HOUSE AND GARDEN

University of Birmingham
58 Edgbaston Park Road, Edgbaston, B15 2RT

A unique heritage experience nestled in a leafy corner of Birmingham, Winterbourne is the botanic garden of the University of Birmingham, adjacent to Edgbaston Pool, a Site of Special Scientific Interest. The garden itself is a seven-acre oasis, home to over 6,000 different plant species, the perfect place to enjoy a peaceful stroll in tranquil surroundings. In the house, visitors can escape the modern world, exploring period rooms filled with antiques and Edwardian era soft furnishings. Learn about the families that lived here and how Winterbourne came to be part of the University of Birmingham.

🌐 winterbourne.org.uk

✉ enquiries@winterbourne.org.uk

Ackers Adventure / ©Ackers Adventure

ACKERS ADVENTURE

Golden Hillock Road, Sparkbrook, B11 2PY

Ackers Adventure is 75 acres of fun for all ages. Only two miles from the centre of Birmingham, visitors can step into open grassland and woodland in this hidden urban oasis. There is so much to choose from – navigate a 100-meter long ski slope or, if you prefer, race down the tobogganing slope instead. Scale the dramatic height of the 25-meter climbing wall and abseiling tower from which you can jump off or zip down. On the water there are canoes, kayaks or bell boats and back on dry land have a go at the nine hole disc golf course or sharpen your aim on the archery range.

🌐 ackers-adventure.co.uk

✉ bookings@ackers-adventure.co.uk

ASTON PARISH CHURCH

Aston Hall Road, Aston, B6 6QA

Aston Parish Church originated in the 9th-century, with the 200ft high spire and tower dating from 1480. Inside the church there are numerous memorials, the earliest from 1360. The Ardens – William Shakespeare's mother's family – owned land in the area and there are three notable Arden tombs and a window. There is also a distinctive bust to John Rogers, an Aston man responsible for the Matthew Bible, the first complete translation from the

original Greek into English. The church is in the Aston Hall and Church conservation area.

🌐 astonnechellscofe.org.uk

✉ sam@astonnechellscofe.org.uk

BIRMINGHAM BUDDHIST VIHARA

29-31 Osler Street, Ladywood, B16 9EU

This golden-domed temple is the only such traditional Burmese style temple in the UK. Founded in 1998, the site is home to the Dhamma Talaka Peace Pagoda, a place of pilgrimage and a resting place for royal relics. Visitors can book a tour of the pagoda and learn about Buddhism. There is also a Dhanma Hall where higher Buddhist teachings occur and a monastery where the monks reside.

🌐 birminghambuddhistvihara.org

✉ venuttaranyana@gmail.com

Birmingham Central Mosque / ©Birmingham Central Mosque

BIRMINGHAM CENTRAL MOSQUE

180 Belgrave Middleway, Highgate, B12 0XS

Birmingham Central Mosque is one of the city's most recognisable religious buildings, and is Britain's second purpose-built mosque, opening to the public in the early 1970s. The mosque welcomes large numbers of visitors from all faiths and cultures each year, providing tours with a faith guide.

🌐 centralmosque.org.uk
✉ visit@centralmosque.org.uk

BIRMINGHAM WILDLIFE CONSERVATION PARK

Birmingham City Council
Pershore Road, Edgbaston, B5 7RL

Birmingham Wildlife Conservation Park is home to a unique collection of animals from across the world, including Red Pandas, lemurs, reptiles, meerkats, otters, birds, wallabies, a large number of monkeys and a Komodo Dragon. With some of the animals endangered in the wild, Birmingham Wildlife Conservation Park plays an important role in the conservation of these species.

🌐 birmingham.gov.uk/info/50042/
    birmingham_ wildlife_conservation_park
✉ bhamconservationpark@birmingham.gov.uk

BOURNVILLE CARILLON

Woodbrooke Road, Bournville, B30 2AA

Commissioned by George Cadbury in 1906 as a gift for the Cadbury workers, and housed within the bell tower of the village school, the

Bournville Carillon / ©Bournville Carillon

Bournville Carillon (a large organ-like instrument consisting of bronze bells) is one of only four 4-octave Carillons in the UK. With 48 bells, Bournville Carillon ranks as one of the finest and largest instruments of its kind and is played regularly throughout the year. Situated in the centre of Bournville Village Green, the historic 'Rest House' – now the Carillon Visitor Centre is also well worth a visit.

🌐 bournvillecarillon.co.uk
✉ info@bournvillecarillon.co.uk

Cadbury World / ©Cadbury World

CADBURY WORLD

Linden Road, Bournville, B30 2LU

Uncover a world of chocolate delights and enjoy a fascinating, fun-packed day out at Cadbury World! You'll learn how your favourite confectionery is made, play in chocolate rain and add your favourite treat to a delicious pot of warm melted Cadbury Dairy Milk. Discover the origins of the cocoa bean before jumping onboard the magical Cadabra ride and meeting the infamous Cadbury drumming gorilla. Plus, join Freddo and a whole host of

Cadbury characters as they whisk you away on an adventurous journey in the 4D Chocolate Adventure cinema experience, complete with motion seats.

🌐 cadburyworld.co.uk

✉ cadburyworldgeneralenquiries@mdlz.com

THE CUSTARD FACTORY
Gibb Street, Digbeth, B9 4AA

Located on the site of the former Bird's Custard factory in Digbeth, the Custard Factory is an independent shopping destination and home to a variety of creative and digital businesses, cafes and bars. The Custard Factory hosts a number of independent markets throughout the year, as well as being one of the best places in the UK for street art.

🌐 digbeth.com

✉ hello@digbeth.com

THE HEART OF BRITAIN'S CANAL NETWORK
Canal & River Trust
Brindleyplace, B1 2AA

With almost 100 miles of canals, Birmingham waterways are the ideal place to unwind in the middle of a busy city. Canals offer something for everyone. If you're looking to be active, there's cycling and canoeing, or if you simply want to relax, there are many vibrant waterfront bars and restaurants to choose from. Admire the historic canal architecture and colourful passing boats while enjoying a cup of coffee or spend a

leisurely afternoon on a tranquil boat trip down the Birmingham Canal.

🌐 canalrivertrust.org.uk/places-to-visit/ birmingham-city-centre

✉ enquiries.westmidlands@canalrivertrust.org.uk

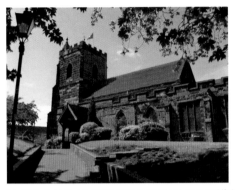

Holy Trinity Parish Church / ©Holy Trinity Parish Church Sutton Coldfield

HOLY TRINITY PARISH CHURCH
Church Hill, Mill Street, Sutton Coldfield, B72 1TF

Holy Trinity Parish Church is Sutton Coldfield's ancient parish church. A church was first recorded at this location as early as the 13th-century and was extended in 1533 by Bishop Vesey, the benefactor of the town. Visitors now can view the ornately painted ceilings, stained glass windows and Bishop Vesey's tomb and learn about the history of the church.

🌐 htsc.org.uk

✉ heritage@htsc.org.uk

J..W.Evans Silver Factory / © English Heritage

J. W. EVANS SILVER FACTORY

English Heritage
54-57 Albion Street, Jewellery Quarter, B1 3EA

Established in 1881, J. W. Evans is one of the most complete surviving historic factories in Birmingham's Jewellery Quarter. Walk into the factory today and visitors enter a lost industrial world. Behind the frontage of four terraced houses, the workshops retain their original drop stamps and fly presses. They are packed with thousands of dies for the manufacture of silverware, as well as the whole of the working equipment, stock and records of the business. Prebooking is essential.

⊕ english-heritage.org.uk/visit/places/j-wevans
silver-factory

✉ CustomerCare@English-Heritage.org.uk

KEY HILL CEMETERY

Key Hill, Jewellery Quarter, B18 5AH

Key Hill was Birmingham's first garden cemetery and was laid out on the site of a

Key Hill Cemetery / ©Anne-Marie Hayes

former sand quarry. It was created in 1836 by a group of non-conformists who objected to paying fees to the Church of England for burial in parish churchyards and the fact their ministers could not conduct funerals there. Key Hill was intended to be a general cemetery open for all denominations. Famous residents include the politician Joseph Chamberlain, Alfred Bird, the manufacturer of Bird's custard, and the poet Constance Naden. Open all year round, dawn to dusk.

⊕ cemeteries.jewelleryquarter.net

Moseley Road Baths / ©Moseley Road Baths

LEGO™ DISCOVERY CENTRE

Merlin Entertainments Group Ltd
Arena, King Edwards Road, Brindleyplace, B1 2AA

Denmark's most famous export, LEGO™, is at the heart of this playground and entertainment centre. Fun for the whole family awaits with a 4D cinema, Kingdom Quest laser ride, DUPLO™ Farm and much more! Discover all of Birmingham's best attractions made from LEGO™ in MINILAND™, and get LEGO™ building tips from the Master Model Builder Workshops.

🌐 legolanddiscoverycentre.com/birmingham
✉ ldc.birmingham@merlinentertainments.biz

MOSELEY ROAD BATHS

497 Moseley Road, Balsall Heath, B12 9BX

A historic community run swimming pool, Moseley Road Baths is a beautiful Grade II Listed building in the heart of Balsall Heath. The baths are a vibrant, sustainable heritage venue offering a range of health, wellbeing and community facilities including swimming.

🌐 moseleyroadbaths.org.uk
✉ keepswimming@moseleyroadbaths.org.uk

THE NATIONAL SEA LIFE CENTRE

Merlin Entertainments Group Ltd
The Water's Edge, Brindleyplace, B1 2HL

The National Sea Life Centre is an aquarium with over 2,000 magical creatures across 60 displays of freshwater and marine life, situated in Brindleyplace. Visit the Penguin Ice Adventure where you can marvel at the cheeky antics of the resident colony of Gentoo penguins! The centre also boasts the UK's only 360° Ocean Tunnel where visitors can come nose to nose with Black Tip Reef sharks, giant rays and resident Giant Green Sea Turtle, Molokai!

🌐 visitsealife.com/birmingham
✉ slcbirmingham@merlinentertainments.biz

OLD RECTORY FARM

Birmingham City Council
Ragley Drive, Church Road, Sheldon, B26 3TU

Situated within Sheldon Country Park, Old Rectory Farm has been fully restored and operates as a demonstration farm, showing traditional agricultural methods. Animals kept at the farm include Jersey cattle, pigs, goats, ponies, ducks, chickens and geese.

🌐 birmingham.gov.uk/parks

THE REVOLUTION WALK

Canal & River Trust
St Vincent Street, Brindleyplace, B16 8EB

The 4.5 mile stretch of the Main Line Canal runs from the Roundhouse in central Birmingham to Chance Glass Works in Smethwick. The Revolution Walk celebrates three eras of transport: canals, railways and roads, evidence of which can be found all along this peaceful and historic canal stretch. Although the Revolution Walk is ideal for discovering more about Birmingham's industrial history, it is also surrounded by leafy banks, trees and even a nature reserve nestling between the New and Old Main Line Canals. There is plenty of wildlife spotting to be done there, including moorhens, geese and herons which are particularly fond of this canal stretch. The flat towpath provides easy access to a wide range of unique heritage and can be used as a green route in and out of the city.

🌐 canalrivertrust.org.uk/places-to-visit/the-revolution-walk

✉ enquiries.westmidlands@canalrivertrust.org.uk

The Revolution Walk / ©Canal & River Trust

Roundhouse Birmingham / ©Jana Eastwood

ROUNDHOUSE BIRMINGHAM
National Trust/ Canal & River Trust
St Vincent Street, Birmingham, B16 8EB

Once canal-side stables and stores, this 19th-century Grade II Listed building has been transformed into a lively hub from which you can explore the city by foot, bike or boat. Created through a landmark partnership between Canal & River Trust and the National Trust, Roundhouse Birmingham is an independent charity, safeguarding the future of this beautiful building by giving it new purpose. Stop by the visitor centre and exhibition space, join a tour or enjoy a drink at the cafe.

🌐 nationaltrust.org.uk/roundhouse-birmingham
   www.roundhousebirmingham.org.uk
✉ hello@roundhousebirmingham.org.uk

St Alban the Martyr / ©S t Alban's PCC

ST ALBAN THE MARTYR
120 Stanhope Street, Highgate, B12 0XB

This Grade II* Listed Victorian Gothic church designed by John Loughborough Pearson, opened in 1881. Within the south chapel is an altarpiece by leading Birmingham Arts and Crafts artists Kate and Myra Bunce. The church opens for heritage events and visitors can take self-led tours of the church and a parish heritage trail.

🌐 saintalban.co.uk
✉ info@stalban.co.uk

St Martin in the Bullring / © St Martin in the Bullring

ST MARTIN IN THE BULLRING
Edgbaston Street, Birmingham, B5 5BB

There has been a church on this site since the 12th-century, the present Grade II Listed Building dating from 1875. The church features a stained glass window by Edward Burne-Jones and is home to the world's first change-ringing peal of 16 bells. It also houses the city's oldest monument, a 1325 effigy of Sir William de Bermingham.

🌐 bullring.org

✉ office@bullring.org

ST PAUL'S CHURCH
St Paul's Square, Jewelley Quarter, B3 1QZ

This Grade I Listed Building is situated in Birmingham's only remaining 18th-century church square. Built in 1779, the church boasts associations with local industrialists Matthew Boulton and James Watt. Housing beautiful stained glass windows, the church's most recent window design is based around the local jewellery trade. The church provides a unique performance space and hosts local community events.

🌐 stpaulsjq.church

✉ enquiries@stpaulsjq.church

St Paul's Church / ©Amy-Rose Photography

St Philips Cathedral / ©Roz Guy

ST PHILIP'S CATHEDRAL
Birmingham Cathedral, Colmore Row, B3 2QB

The Cathedral Church of Saint Philip is the Church of England cathedral and the seat of the Bishop of Birmingham. Built as a parish church and consecrated in 1715, St Philip's became the cathedral of the newly formed Diocese of Birmingham in 1905. A Grade I Listed Building, the cathedral is is a rare and fine example of elegant English Baroque architecture and one of the oldest buildings in the city still used for its original purpose. The cathedral is home to some remarkable treasures (not least the inspiring stained-glass windows designed by Edward Burne-Jones) and amazing stories, all set amongst the daily rhythm of people criss-crossing this unique part of the city.

🌐 birminghamcathedral.com
✉ enquiries@birminghamcathedral.com

STIRCHLEY BATHS COMMUNITY HUB
2-4 Bournville Lane, Stirchley, B30 2JT

Former historic and heritage swimming pool, the baths have been transformed into a hub at the heart of the community, Hosting an exciting programme of community activities and events, including heritage tours, film screenings and family trails around the building, there is also an onsite cafe space offering teas and coffees.

🌐 stirchleybaths.org
✉ hello@stirchleybaths.org

WARSTONE LANE CEMETERY
Warstone Lane, Jewellery Quarter, B18 6LJ

This Church of England cemetery opened in 1848 and is best known for the unique two-tiered circular catacombs in the centre, where many of Birmingham's elite were interred including John Baskerville, the printer who created the Baskerville typeface in 1757. Elsewhere in the cemetery, notable names include Major Harry Gem, the lawn tennis pioneer and William Edward Hipkins who died when the Titanic sank in 1912. Open all year round, dawn to dusk.

🌐 cemeteries.jewelleryquarter.net

Warstone Lane Cemetery / ©Anne-Marie Hayes

Birmingham Hippodrome / ©Birmingham Hippodrome

THE ALEXANDRA

Suffolk Street Queensway, Birmingham, B5 4DS

Originally the Lyceum Theatre when it first opened in 1901, the Alexandra Theatre has become home to first class entertainment throughout its history. In 2018, the venue underwent an extensive refurbishment. The theatre is a valuable contributor to culture within Birmingham and the West Midlands, presenting first-rate musicals, drama, comedy and more to a wide audience.

🌐 atgtickets.com/birmingham

✉ birminghamstagedoor@theambassadors.com

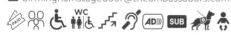

BIRMINGHAM HIPPODROME

Hurst Street, Southside, B5 4TB

Located in the Chinese Quarter, Birmingham Hippodrome is a cultural hub that gives everyone the chance to experience unforgettable theatrical performances, arts and culture. Home to Birmingham Royal Ballet, DanceXchange and DanceHub, the Hippodrome's two stages also showcase world-class musicals, opera, dance, pantomime and drama. Hippodrome Festivals produce spectacular outdoor arts and festivals. With a regular annual attendance of over 600,000, the Hippodrome is one of the busiest single theatres in the United Kingdom.

🌐 birminghamhippodrome.com

✉ info@birminghamhippodrome.com

The Alexandra Theatre / ©The Alexandra Theatre

BIRMINGHAM REPERTORY THEATRE

6 Centenary Square, Birmingham, B1 2EP

Birmingham Repertory Theatre is the only producing theatre in the England's Second City. The oldest building-based theatre company in the UK, The REP has an unparalleled pioneering history and has been at the forefront of theatre in the UK for over 100 years. The REP's mission is to create artistically ambitious popular theatre for, by and with the people of Birmingham and the wider world. The commissioning and production of new work lies at the core of The REP's programme and over the last 15 years, the company has produced more than 130 new plays. As well as presenting over 60 productions on its three stages every year, the theatre tours its productions nationally and internationally.

🌐 birmingham-rep.co.uk
✉ ticketservices@birmingham-rep.co.uk

THE BLUE ORANGE THEATRE

118 Great Hampton Street, Jewellery Quarter, B18 6AD

The Blue Orange Theatre is an independent venue located in the heart of Birmingham's world famous Jewellery Quarter. The theatre is operated by JW Theatres, a company founded on the idea of high quality theatre presented at an affordable cost. From staged concerts to intimate plays, from dance schools to full scale musical theatre; the Blue Orange Theatre aims to be a home for all. Facilities include a 108 seat main house theatre with a flexible rehearsal studio, the theatres bar offers a welcoming environment ideal for meeting for a coffee or trying one of the venues' themed cocktails.

🌐 blueorangetheatre.co.uk
✉ info@jwtheatres.co.uk

Birmingham Rep / ©Ross Jukes

Digbeth Arena / ©Brian Wilson

THE CRESCENT THEATRE
20 Sheepcote Street, Brindleyplace, B16 8AE

As a long-established arts venue, the Crescent Theatre is highly regarded as one of Birmingham's oldest theatre companies, producing high quality productions. Operating from a purpose-built theatre in Brindleyplace, the theatre has a 300+ seat main house, 100+ seat studio theatre, rehearsal rooms and spacious bar.

🌐 crescent-theatre.co.uk
✉ boxoffice@crescent-theatre.co.uk

DIGBETH ARENA
Lower Trinity Street, Deritend, B9 4AG

Digbeth Arena is a unique, open-air venue, just a short walk from central Birmingham. It hosts live music events and regular club nights, along with regular award-winning street food events at weekends.

🌐 digbetharena.com
✉ enquiries@tegmjr.com

The Crescent Theatre / ©The Crescent Theatre

THE ELECTRIC CINEMA
47-49, Station Street, Birmingham, B5 4DY

The Electric is a historic cinema and sound recording facility. It opened in Station Street in 1909, showing its first silent film on 27 December of that year, and is now the oldest working cinema in the country. The cinema has two screens, with licensed bar, showing the best in quality mainstream and independent films.

 theelectric.co.uk

 info@theelectric.co.uk

Everyman Cinema / ©Everyman Cinemas

EVERYMAN CINEMA
116 Wharfside Street, The Mailbox, B1 1RF

With a wide array of mainstream, independent and classic films, special events, launches and a diverse calendar of live satellite broadcasts, there is something for everyone at Everyman. Everyman Cinemas look to provide an innovative lifestyle approach to their venues, where you swap your soft drink for a nice glass of red wine and a slice of freshly made pizza served to your seat, creating a warm and friendly atmosphere, in a luxurious cinematic experience. Everyman Mailbox Birmingham has three screens with armchair seating and footrests, and offers a full food and drink menu, where you can have a drink or order hot food or snacks in the foyer bars.

 everymancinema.com/mailbox-birmingham

talk@everymangroup.com

The Electric Cinema / ©The Electric Cinema

THE GLEE CLUB
The Arcadian, 70 Hurst Street, Southside, B5 4TD

First opened in 1994, the Glee Club is an award-winning live comedy and music venue, staging regular stand-up nights and intimate music shows, with dining. Situated in Southside, Birmingham, the Glee's home, the Arcadian

The Glee Club / ©Jack Spicer Adams

was the first dedicated comedy club to open in the UK outside London. The venue is home to several unique award-winning comedy shows and many noteable local comics have graced the Glee's stage, including Guz Khan, Jasper Carrott, Joe Lycett and Lenny Henry.

🌐 glee.co.uk/birmingham
✉ info@glee.co.uk

HARE AND HOUNDS
106 High Street, Kings Heath, B14 7JZ

Situated in south Birmingham, the Hare and Hounds is a Grade II Listed Building, and features beautiful and unique Art Nouveau tiles that line the entry hall and staircase. Since 2007 the pub has established itself as one of the most important and influential live music venues in the country, playing a vital part in nurturing the city's vibrant music and creative community. The pub boasts two downstairs bars which host a weekly pub quiz on Wednesdays, the hugely popular Blues Club on Saturday afternoons, comedy workshops and more. The two famous upstairs venues feature live music and club nights

Hare and Hounds / ©Hare and Hounds

spanning jazz, indie, funk, reggae, hip hop, soul, house, techno, drum & bass and beyond.

🌐 hareandhoundskingsheath.co.uk
✉ matt@leftfootvenues.co.uk

HIGHBURY THEATRE CENTRE
Sheffield Road, Sutton Coldfield, B73 5HD

Highbury Theatre is a non-professional theatre situated in the royal town of Sutton Coldfield, It is one of the oldest, established amateur theatres in the city and a founding member of the Little Theatre Guild of Great Britain.

🌐 highburytheatre.co.uk
✉ admin1@highburytheatre.co.uk

Midlands Art Centre / ©Kate Green

LEGACY CENTRE OF EXCELLENCE
144 Potters Lane, Aston, B6 4UU

Legacy Centre of Excellence, formerly the Drum Arts Centre, is Europe's largest centre for Black-owned business and arts. Based in Aston, one of Birmingham's most diverse communities, it is dedicated to raising aspirations for the community, local people and businesses alike. The venue offers a range of events, workshops and projects to encourage engagement with the arts, STEM and business within the local community. The Legacy Centre of Excellence has been re-established as a venue for world-class local and international live music across a range of genres, and has a flexible space for performance art, exhibitions and shows.

🌐 legacycoe.co.uk
✉ info@legacycoe.co.uk

MIDLANDS ARTS CENTRE (MAC)
Cannon Hill Park, Birmingham, B12 9QH

Located in Cannon Hill Park, just two miles south of the city centre, the MAC attracts over 1,000,000 visits every year, drawing audiences from across the UK and beyond. Specialising in contemporary work, MAC offers audiences a busy programme of theatre and performance, independent cinema, exhibitions and creative practical courses – from ceramics to digital photography. Midlands Arts Centre is a national leader in developing work with children, families and young people of all backgrounds. Working both in the state-of-the-art building and out in the community, the MAC's mission is to make art an important part of people's lives.

🌐 macbirmingham.co.uk
✉ info@macbirmingham.co.uk

THE MILL

29 Lower Trinity Street, Digbeth, B9 4AG

A multi-purpose event space and club venue in Digbeth; offering a mezzanine warehouse and Birmingham's favourite open-top roof garden situated against the Victorian railway arches. This club hosts a selection of nights with varied live music and other performances.

🌐 themilldigbeth.com

✉ enquiries@tegmjr.com

ODEON LUXE BIRMINGHAM BROADWAY PLAZA

220 Ladywood Middleway, Birmingham, B16 8LP

With 12 luxury screens including a state-of-the-art iSense screen, all with stunning RealD 3D. Every seat on every row at ODEON Luxe Birmingham Broadway Plaza has been expertly designed to allow visitors to recline and relax while watching a film.

🌐 odeon.co.uk

ODEON BIRMINGHAM NEW STREET

139 New Street, Birmingham, B2 4NU

Situated in the heart of the city centre, ODEON Birmingham New Street features eight screens showing the latest film releases for all ages. Visitors can also experience the magic of cinema in RealD 3D.

🌐 odeon.co.uk

THE OLD JOINT STOCK PUB AND THEATRE

4 Temple Row West, Birmingham, B2 5NY

Built in 1862, the Grade II Listed Building that houses the Old Joint Stock was originally designed as a library before becoming the Birmingham Joint Stock Bank. Situated opposite St Philip's Cathedral, the building is now a stunning pub, and is also home to the Old Joint

The Old Joint Stock Pub and Theatre / ©Old Joint Stock

Stock Theatre, a professional 100 seat studio theatre, perfect for intimate performances. It has a busy programme of shows and features everything from new writing to musical theatre cabaret nights and top quality fringe theatre.

🌐 oldjointstock.co.uk

✉ oldjointstock@fullers.co.uk

THE OLD REP THEATRE

45 Station Street, Birmingham B5 4DY

The Old Rep (previously known as Birmingham Repertory Theatre) first opened its doors in 1913 and occupies a unique place in theatre history as Britain's first purpose-built repertory theatre. Throughout its history the Old Rep has played a central role in the early careers of many of the nation's most celebrated actors and theatre makers.

🌐 oldreptheatre.co.uk

✉ info@oldreptheatre.co.uk

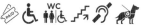

ROYAL BIRMINGHAM CONSERVATOIRE

Birmingham City University
Birmingham City University, 200 Jennens Road, B4 7XR

The Royal Birmingham Conservatoire is a music school, drama school and concert venue. From great music to captivating speakers, there's something for everyone on the Conservatoire events calendar. With its £57 million teaching and performance facility the Royal Birmingham Conservatoire is the first of its kind in the digital age and is the perfect fusion of traditional and contemporary.

🌐 bcu.ac.uk/conservatoire

✉ conservatoire@bcu.ac.uk

Royal Birmingham Conservatoire / ©Royal Birmingham Conservatoire

Sutton Coldfield Town Hall / ©Mike Wade

SUTTON ARTS THEATRE
South Parade, Sutton Coldfield, B72 1QU

This amateur theatre venue is renowned for its high quality, award- winning productions and each season provides a variety of dramatic productions to suit all tastes including plays, pantomimes and musicals.

🌐 suttonartstheatre.co.uk
✉ info@suttonartstheatre.co.uk

SUTTON COLDFIELD TOWN HALL
Upper Clifton Road, Sutton Coldfield, B73 6DA

Sutton Coldfield Town Hall is a Grade A Locally Listed Building of inimitable character and regal charm. Over the course of its existence and evolution, the Town Hall has at one time or other functioned either solely or simultaneously as a; hotel, hospital, theatre, meeting place for councillors and even, for a time, fire station. Sutton Coldfield Town Hall now regularly plays host to a spectrum of events, from household name comedy shows and theatrical productions to much more. It also provides facilities for entertainment, education, community gatherings, recreation and leisure activities.

🌐 suttoncoldfieldtownhall.com
✉ enquiries@suttoncoldfieldtownhall.com

Symphony Hall / ©Mike Gutteridge

SYMPHONY HALL BIRMINGHAM

THSH
The International Convention Centre,
Broad Street, B1 2EA

Symphony Hall is widely considered one of the finest concert halls in the world. Set in the bustling heart of Birmingham, the venue is home to the City of Birmingham Symphony Orchestra and also hosts the best in jazz, world music, folk, rock, pop and stand-up comedy. An architectural triumph and one of the world's best concert halls acoustically, Symphony Hall is built in the traditional shoebox shape of the great 19th-century halls, but with innovations developed by renowned acoustic consultant Russell Johnson.

🌐 thsh.co.uk
✉ boxoffice@thsh.co.uk

TOWN HALL BIRMINGHAM

THSH
Victoria Square, Birmingham B3 3DQ

As one of the city's most well-loved historic buildings, situated in the iconic Victoria Square, the Town Hall has been a hub of Birmingham's civic and cultural life for more than 180 years. This Grade I Listed Building hosts everything from classical to comedy to rock to pop, and is now one of the city's most versatile venues having featured artists such as David Bowie, Led Zeppelin, Tony Iommi, Caitlin Moran and more. Famous classical premieres include Mendelssohn's *Elijah* and Elgar's *The Dream of Gerontius, The Apostles, The Kingdom* and *The Music Makers.*

🌐 thsh.co.uk
✉ boxoffice@thsh.co.uk

UTILITA ARENA BIRMINGHAM

NEC Group
King Edwards Rd, Brindleyplace, B1 2AA

Since first opening in 1991 The Utilitia Arena has built a reputation as a versatile and experienced venue, hosting concerts, sporting events, conferences, family shows and much more. Home to everything from record breaking sports to world class family entertainment; from the latest pop sensations to side splitting comedy from some of the world's best comics, Utilita Arena Birmingham is bigger and better than ever bringing you events you won't want to forget!

🌐 utilitaarenabham.co.uk

Town Hall / ©Simon Hadley

ASTON PARK

Birmingham City Council

Trinity Road, Aston, B6 6JD

This magnificent Green Flag Award winning park forms an idyllic setting for a Jacobean mansion Aston Hall, providing a backdrop of mature trees and shrubs, sweeping avenues and constantly changing planting schemes. Aston Hall and Park are a focal point for community events, from Aston Pride to a mini-Olympics for local school children.

🌐 birmingham.gov.uk/parks

BALAAM'S WOOD LOCAL NATURE RESERVE

Birmingham City Council

Balaams Wood Drive, Rubery, Birmingham, B31 5HF

Balaam's Wood Local Nature Reserve is made up of 6.5 acres of ancient oak woodland a similar amount of grassland. The River Rea runs through the reserve.

🌐 birmingham.gov.uk/parks

Aston Park / ©Birmingham Museums Trust

Birmingham Botanical Gardens / ©Birmingham Botanical Gardens

BIRMINGHAM BOTANICAL GARDENS

Westbourne Road, Edgbaston, B15 3TR

With the character of a charming Victorian public park, complete with bandstand, Birmingham Botanical Gardens offers something for everyone, be it one of the four stunning glasshouses showing tropical rainforest or arid desert, playground, tearoom and garden or gift shop all surrounded by some of the most beautiful gardens in the UK. There is also a large lawn in front of the glasshouses with a range of beds and shrubberies.

🌐 birminghambotanicalgardens.org.uk
✉ admin@birminghambotanicalgardens.org.uk

BOURNVILLE PARK

Birmingham City Council
Selly Oak Road, Bournville, B30 1UG

Located within Bournville Village, facilities include a play area and large open area. Bourn Brook runs through the park.

🌐 birmingham.gov.uk/parks

Bournville Village Green / ©Bournville Village Trust

BOURNVILLE VILLAGE GREEN

Bournville Village Trust
Linden Road, Bournville, B30 1JT

A beautiful green space located in the centre of Bournville, the Village Green dates back to 1900 and was part of chocolate-maker George Cadbury's original plans for the garden village. Today, it regularly plays host to some of Bournville's most popular events, including the Christmas Eve carol service and the Christmas lights switch on. Also home to the Grade II Listed Bournville Rest House which was built in 1914 to celebrate the silver wedding anniversary of George and Elizabeth Cadbury and paid for by Cadbury workers, the green is situated round the corner from Selly Manor Museum. Bournville Green is also a Green Flag Award winner.

🌐 bvt.org.uk
✉ enquiries@bvt.org.uk

BROMWICH WOOD LOCAL NATURE RESERVE

Birmingham City Council
Scotland Lane, Birmingham, B32 4BT

Situated immediately northeast of Bartley Reservoir, with a connecting footpath to Woodgate Valley Country Park, Bromwich Wood Local Nature Reserve contains a large and diverse plant community. Mainly comprised of English oak trees, there are also sweet chestnut, sessile oak, wild cherry, alder and rowan. During the spring a large numbers of bluebells flower and a variety of species of birds can be seen in the wood.

🌐 birmingham.gov.uk/parks

Bromwich Wood / ©Birmingham Museums Trust

BROOKVALE PARK

Birmingham City Council
Park Road, Birmingham, B23 7YT

Based around a large lake, Brookvale Park is home to a bowling green, tennis courts, a play area and a sailing club.

🌐 birmingham.gov.uk/parks

BURBURY BRICKWORKS RIVER WALK

Birmingham City Council
Sparkhill, Birmingham, B11 3AX

A 13-acre river walk situated on the site of a former brickmaking factory that existed until the early 1960s, Burbury Brickworks is also part of the Shire Country Park. The River Cole runs around one edge of the park. When the brickworks closed the land began to return to its natural state. There are now areas of marshland and young oak trees.

🌐 birmingham.gov.uk/parks

CANNON HILL PARK

Birmingham City Council
Russell Road, Moseley, B13 8RD

Made up of 80 acres of formal parkland and 120 acres of conservation and woodland plantation, Cannon Hill Park is also home to the Birmingham Wildlife Conservation Centre and the MAC theatre. A Green Flag Award winner, the park also features two children's play areas; a children's mini fun-fair; fishing facilities; a 36

hole mini golf course in the park; pedalo boats for hire during the summer season; and tennis courts.

🌐 birmingham.gov.uk/parks

CASTLE VALE CENTRE PARK

Birmingham City Council
Tangmere Drive, Castle Vale, B35 6QS

Green Flag Award winning Castle Vale Centre Park covers just under six acres of parkland, featuring a formal garden and seating area, along with ornamental and non-ornamental gardens and a dedicated conservation areas. There are play facilities for children of different ages, multi-use pitches for football, basketball and other games, as well as space for events. A special area is devoted to ornamental grasses, predominantly *Lolium perenne* (Perennial Rye Grass) and *Poa annua* (Annual Meadow Grass).

🌐 birmingham.gov.uk/parks

COFTON PARK

Birmingham City Council
Cofton Park, Northfield, B45 8UN

Cofton Park is 135 acres of rolling fields and trees and is situated on the slopes adjoining Lickey Hills Country Park. The park is mainly made up of open grassland, and has football pitches for use by the local community. The centre of the park features a small woodland area. Stunning oak and ash trees flourish and mark what was once a boundary of Lowhill Farm.

🌐 birmingham.gov.uk/parks

Cotteridge Park / ©Birmingham Museums Trust

EASTSIDE CITY PARK
Birmingham City Council
Curzon Street, Birmingham, B4 7AP

Eastside City Park is a 6.75 acre urban park in Birmingham city centre. Green Flag Award winning, the park boasts landscaped green space, hundreds of trees, a large canal water feature and a public square with jet fountains. The park is located next to Millennium Point, which is home to Thinktank, and features a toddlers' playground.

 birmingham.gov.uk/parks

COTTERIDGE PARK
Birmingham City Council
Franklin Road, Birmingham, B30 2HE

A 22-acre Victorian park boasting a Green Flag Award, facilities at Cotteridge Park include a playground, basketball courts, skate park and tennis courts. There is also a walking route through the park.

 birmingham.gov.uk/parks

EDGBASTON RESERVOIR
Birmingham City Council
115 Reservoir Road, Ladywood, B16 9EE

This 70-acre site is mainly open water. The reservoir is surrounded by woodland and grassland. Walkers and joggers can enjoy the 1.75 mile trail around the reservoir. The area supports a variety of birdlife and is a valuable city site for animals such as newts and bats.

 birmingham.gov.uk/parks

Edgbaston Resevoir / ©Birmingham Museums Trust

Grove Park / ©Birmingham Museums Trust

GROVE PARK

Birmingham City Council
253 Harborne Park Rd, Birmingham, B17 0BJ

The park was historically the grounds of The Grove, an 18th-century Georgian house. One of Birmingham's first MPs, Thomas Attwood, lived at The Grove between 1823 and 1846. This quiet park in Harborne has a lake, large playing fields and a popular children's play area with plenty to do. It has large climbing frames that allow your youngsters to enjoy the view over Birmingham.

🌐 birmingham.gov.uk/parks

HANDSWORTH PARK

Birmingham City Council
Holly Road, Handsworth, B20 2BY

Handsworth Park is a Green Flag Award winning park with over 63 acres of landscaped grass slopes, flower beds, mature trees, shrubs, and plenty of wildlife. Handsworth Leisure Centre is based in the park. There is also a boating lake, and the park hosts a variety of both council and community organised events – from Vaisakhi

with its huge processions to the Marcus Garvey Festival with music and entertainment.

🌐 birmingham.gov.uk/parks

Handsworth Park/ ©Birmingham Museums Trust

HIGHBURY PARK

Birmingham City Council
Shutlock Lane, Kings Heath, B13 8QG

Highbury Park is located on the borders between Moseley and Kings Heath. Highbury Hall, the former residence of politician Joseph Chamberlain, is on the northern edge of the park.

🌐 birmingham.gov.uk/parks

Highbury Park / ©Birmingham Museums Trust

Jones Woods / ©Birmingham Museums Trust

Hill Hook Nature Reserve / ©Birmingham Museums Trust

HILL HOOK NATURE RESERVE

Birmingham City Council
Netherstone Grove, Sutton Coldfield, B74 4XF

Located in Four Oaks, Hill Hook Local Nature Reserve has a wide variety of habitats ranging from grassland, scrub and dry woodland to open water. The large pool on the nature reserve originally provided water to Hill Hook Corn Mill.

🌐 birmingham.gov.uk/parks

JONES WOODS

Fox Hollies Road, Sutton Coldfield, B76 2RD

This ancient woodland area in the heart of Walmley, Jones Wood, measures almost six acres of mature deciduous woodland made up largely of oak and birch with beech and sycamore. Old boundary banks and ditches are still evident here, as are old pollards and coppice stools.

🌐 birmingham.gov.uk/parks

KINGFISHER COUNTRY PARK

Birmingham City Council
Cole Valley Road, Birmingham, B28 0DG

Kingfisher Country Park was opened in 2004. It was created to care for an 6.5mile stretch of the River Cole valley. The valley contains many different types of landscapes and wildlife habitats. Alongside the river there are areas of formal public open space, tall herbs and scrub, coarse grassland, wetland with several small ponds and ancient woodland and there are several artificial lakes in the park. The lake at Shard End has been created in the remains of an old gravel quarry, while Babbs Mill Lake in Kingshurst was formed as a balancing feature in times of flood.

🌐 birmingham.gov.uk/parks

KINGS HEATH PARK

Birmingham City Council
Vicarage Road, Kings Heath, B14 7TQ

Kings Heath Park covers around 35 acres. It was the first urban park in Birmingham to achieve Green Flag Award status. Facilities include a tearoom, bowling green, plant nursery and two playgrounds. The park contains a diverse mix of vegetation and habitats with woodland plantation. There is a seasonal programme which includes outdoor fun events for families, craft activities, guided walks, practical conservation days and training courses. Visitors can also go on guided walks and talks for local community groups.

🌐 birmingham.gov.uk/parks

Kingsbury Water Park / ©Warwickshire County Parks

KINGSBURY WATER PARK
Warwickshire Country Parks
Bodymoor Heath, Sutton Coldfield, B76 0DY

Situated in over 600 acres of stunning country park, Kingsbury Water Park is comprised of 15 separate lakes. Enjoy a picnic in the park, take a ride on the miniature railway or enjoy a stroll along the paths and explore all the hidden corners and wildlife that the wonders of nature have created. Spot birds from numerous hides overlooking the lake, or explore one of the two adventure play areas.

🌐 countryparks.warwickshire.gov.uk
✉ parks@warwickshire.gov.uk

KINGS NORTON PARK
Birmingham City Council
Wychall Lane, Kings Norton, B30 3EP

This Green Flag Award winning park offers an open green space with features including a children's playground and a skate park. There is also a walking trail through the park.

🌐 birmingham.gov.uk/parks

LICKEY HILLS COUNTRY PARK
Birmingham City Council
Warren Lane, Lickey, B45 8ER

Lickey Hills Country Park is one of Birmingham's most varied and treasured parks, covering 524 acres and is located just 10 miles south west of the city centre. A place for family days out, to spot wildlife, for sport, or maybe just for the views and a cup of tea, Lickey Hills has a complex and interesting geology which has created a variety of habitats. These include woodland, heathland, and grassland, which are home to an incredible diversity of wildlife. Lickey Hills has a Green Flag Award and is accredited as a Country Park. There's a children's adventure playground and free table-tennis near the visitor centre. The Country Park has several marked walking trails of varying lengths and difficulty. At Beacon Hill there is a toposcope in a small 'fort' which points out the direction to notable landscape features you can see from the top of the hill. On a clear day points in 13 old counties can be seen.

🌐 birmingham.gov.uk/parks

MANOR FARM PARK
Birmingham City Council
Bristol Road South, Northfield, B31 2AB

Manor Farm Park is a 50-acre open space with woodlands, meadows and a lake with numerous walking trails. The park also features a children's play area, nature trails and a wildlife corridor.

🌐 birmingham.gov.uk/parks

Lickey Hills / ©Birmingham Museums Trust

MARTINEAU GARDENS
27 Priory Road, Edgbaston, B5 7UG

Martineau Gardens is a community space in Edgbaston, featuring over two acres of woodland and formal gardens to explore. A beautiful therapeutic garden, Martineau Gardens provides an oasis for wildlife, a haven of tranquillity, and a destination for an outdoor escape. Garden highlights include an orchard growing figs, mulberries, grapes and apples; demonstration vegetable and herb beds; a woodland home to Pipistrelle bats, badgers and birds and many species of fungi; nature trail; children's play area; wildflower meadows; bird hide; ponds; beehives; and earth oven.

🌐 martineau-gardens.org.uk

✉ info@martineau-gardens.org.uk

MOONLIT PARK AND SUNSET PARK
Birmingham City Council
Bell Barn Road, Birmingham, B15 2AF

The Green Flag Award winning Sunset and Moonlit Parks were designed as part of a local regeneration project. Moonlit Park is home to a play area for children and a wildflower meadow, while Sunset Park hosts an outdoor events space.

🌐 birmingham.gov.uk/parks

MOSELEY BOG
Birmingham City Council
Wake Green Road, Moseley, B13 9YP

Moseley Bog is on the site of an old millpond. It is made up of both wet and dry woodland together with patches of fen vegetation which has developed on the site of the millpond.

Martineau Gardens / © Martineau Gardens

Moseley Bog / ©Birmingham Museums Trust

Joy's Wood is an area of secondary woodland, which has developed on the old gardens along the eastern boundary. Moseley Bog is part of the Shire Country Park. JRR Tolkien lived nearby as a child and acknowledged the site as inspiration for the ancient forests in his books *The Lord of the Rings* and *The Hobbit*. The site also has archaeological interest. It has two burnt mounds which date back to the Bronze Age which are designated as Scheduled Ancient Monuments. There are also more recent remains such as the old mill dam and the foundations of Victorian greenhouses.

🌐 birmingham.gov.uk/parks

MOSELEY PARK AND POOL
93B Alcester Road, Moseley, B13 8DD

Less than two miles from Birmingham city centre and unaltered for over a hundred years lies 11 acres of peaceful parkland, a beautiful lake packed with fish and water fowl and surrounded by trees. This historic park was originally a major part of the gardens of the Moseley Hall estate which were designed by the famous landscape gardener Humphry Repton. Towards the end of the 19th-century much of the estate was being sold for house building. Realising that it was only a matter of time before the remaining part of the gardens would be built upon, a group of far sighted businessmen bought the park and pool in order to preserve it for the citizens of Birmingham. It is a green tranquil oasis that is a haven for wildlife. Its popularity continues to grow not only within Birmingham, but also nationally due to the continuing success of the Jazz and Folk festivals.

🌐 moseleypark.co.uk
✉ info@moseleypark.co.uk

Moseley Park & Pool / ©Birmingham Museums Trust

New Hall Valley Country Park / ©Birmingham Museums Trust

NEW HALL VALLEY COUNTRY PARK

Birmingham City Council
Wylde Green Road, Sutton Coldfield, B76 1NL

This former farmland covers 198 acres of green belt countryside. It is an important nature reserve consisting of historic wetland, grazing meadows, Plants Brook stream and a number of listed buildings.

🌐 birmingham.gov.uk/parks

OLD YARDLEY PARK

Birmingham City Council
off Queens Road, Yardley, B33 8PB

This small village green space, situated a short walk from Blakesley Hall, offers a recreation space and features a children's play area.

🌐 birmingham.gov.uk/parks

PERRY HALL PARK

Birmingham City Council
Perry Avenue, Birmingham, B42 1RS

Situated on the former site of an Elizabethan mansion, ornamental gardens and parkland, Perry Hall Park's 158-acre Green Flag Award winning site is divided by the River Tame. To the south west is the home of the Birmingham Cricket League with 15 cricket pitches and to the north east is the area known as Perry Hall Park. The park is predominantly grassland with a patchwork of trees and wooded areas as well as stretches of hedgerow. There are two wildflower meadows where a variety of orchids can be seen early summer. Perry Hall Park is also home to the Monarchs Cycle Speedway.

🌐 birmingham.gov.uk/parks

Perry Hall Park / ©Birmingham Museums Trust

Plantsbrook Nature Reserve / ©Birmingham Museums Trust

PERRY PARK

Birmingham City Council
Perry Avenue, Birmingham, B42 1RP

Perry Park is home to Alexander Stadium and Perry Reservoir. The Birmingham BMX racetrack, built for the 2012 BMX World Championships is also based in the park. The BMX club based at the track runs a range of activities, from school groups and birthday parties to structured coaching sessions and Olympic athlete training. You can fish in Perry Park and there are two varied walking routes marked out within the park.

🌐 birmingham.gov.uk/parks

PLANTSBROOK NATURE RESERVE

Birmingham City Council
Eachelhurst Road, Erdington, B76 1DZ

Plantsbrook Local Nature Reserve has a number of pools, surrounded by fringes of woodland, wetlands, and a wildflower meadow, making it an oasis for wildlife. A large proportion of the 26-acre site is open water. The site lies on the Plantsbrook wildlife corridor, as does the nearby Hall Valley Country Park. Plantsbrook was purchased by the city and saved from development and was designated a Local Nature Reserve in 1991.

🌐 birmingham.gov.uk/parks

Pype Hayes Park / ©Birmingham Museums Trust

PYPE HAYES PARK

Birmingham City Council
Chester Road, Erdington, B24 0NR

Pype Hayes is one of the largest parks in Birmingham and covers over 100 acres. The park contains a number of ornamental gardens, with many bedding areas.

🌐 birmingham.gov.uk/parks

QUEEN'S PARK

Birmingham City Council
Court Oak Road, Harborne, B17 9AH

Opened in 1898 to celebrate Queen Victoria's diamond jubilee, the park features a children's playground, tennis courts and a large open green space for recreation.

🌐 birmingham.gov.uk/parks

ROOKERY PARK

Birmingham City Council
Western Road, Erdington, B24 9SE

Situated in the grounds of Rookery House, the park features an Italian sunken garden, woodlands and a children's play area. This urban green space offering recreational facilities including tennis courts, and a walking trail.

🌐 birmingham.gov.uk/parks

RECTORY PARK

Birmingham City Council
Broomie Close, Sutton Coldfield, B75 7SF

Rectory Park is home to Sutton Coldfield's main football park. The remaining parkland is natural and contains mature woodland and wild grassland areas. Parts of the park are leased to the Sutton Cricket and Hockey Club and Sutton United Football Club.

🌐 birmingham.gov.uk/parks

ROWHEATH PAVILION AND PARK

Trinity Christian Centre Limited
Heath Road, Bournville, B30 1HH

Rowheath Park is a popular family park with Rowheath Pavilion that is used by a variety of community groups and sports clubs for all ages including football, rugby and athletics. Part of the pavilion became a Grade II Listed Building in 2017. Facilities include a cafe and children's play area. The park also regularly hosts street food events, craft fairs and food and drink festivals.

🌐 rowheathpavilion.co.uk
✉ info@rowheathpavilion.co.uk

Rowheath Pavilion and Park / ©Jay@jayjayjetplane

Sheldon Country Park / ©Birmingham Museums Trust

RUBERY CUTTINGS LOCAL NATURE RESERVE

Birmingham City Council
Leach Green Lane, Northfield, B45 9JL

Rubery Cuttings is an important geological site in Birmingham. Fossils can be found in some of the beds of the Rubery Sandstone. In order to go to the site, visits must be pre-arranged. You can do this by contacting the Local Nature Reserves officer or the Ranger Service at the Lickey Hill Country Park. Rubery Cuttings was declared a Local Nature Reserve in 1991.

🌐 birmingham.gov.uk/parks

SELLY OAK PARK

Birmingham City Council
Gibbins Road, Selly Oak, B29 6SS

With 30 acres of medieval deer park, Selly Oak Park is the largest public park in the Selly Oak district. With a Green Flag Award, a playground

and walking routes through the park, the area provides a peaceful oasis in a busy part of the city.

🌐 birmingham.gov.uk/parks

SHELDON COUNTRY PARK

Birmingham City Council
Ragley Drive, Church Road, Sheldon, B26 3TU

Sheldon Country Park covers an area of just over 300 acres. It is made up of open grassland, wetlands, old hedgerows and some mature woodland. The Old Rectory Farm is open to visitors throughout the year. The park includes a playground near the main entrance off Ragley Drive, picnic area, and three marked football pitches.

🌐 birmingham.gov.uk/parks

Sutton Park / ©Birmingham Museums Trust

SHIRE COUNTRY PARK

Birmingham City Council
Colebank Road, Birmingham, B13 0BD

Shire Country Park is a Local Nature Reserve south of the city centre that follows the River Cole valley for four miles and crosses one of the few remaining fords in the city. The park contains wetlands, grasslands, woodland, and heath, which all support a wealth of animal and plant life. The park was named to honour the life and work of JRR Tolkien who lived within its borders as a young child. Tolkien's childhood adventures in the park are said to have inspired some of his literary works. The park includes a number of sites including Sarehole Mill, Moseley Bog, Trittiford Mill Pool and Burbury Brickworks.

🌐 birmingham.gov.uk/parks

SUTTON PARK

Birmingham City Council
Park Road, Sutton Coldfield, B73 6BU

Sutton Park is a 2,400-acre National Nature Reserve located six miles north of the city centre. It's one of the largest urban parks in Europe and is designated as a Site of Special Scientific Interest and a Scheduled Ancient Monument. The park has open heathland, woodlands, seven lakes, wetlands, and marshes – each with its own rich variety of plants and wildlife, some rarely seen in the region. Cattle and wild ponies graze on the land. There are two children's playground in the park. There are also dozens of paths and bridleways, making it easy to explore the park. Fishing is permitted in Blackroot, Bracebridge, Powells and Keepers

Pools and there are two orienteering courses, with maps available from the visitor centre.

🌐 birmingham.gov.uk/parks

SWANSHURST PARK

Birmingham City Council
Yardley Wood Road, Kings Heath, B13 0TB

Much of Swanhurst Park is natural heathland, making the park an important nature conservation habitat for the city. There are two large pools within the park that are both very good sites for waterfowl.

🌐 birmingham.gov.uk/parks

TRITTIFORD MILL PARK

Birmingham City Council
Priory Road, Yardley Wood, B28 0TB

Once the site of a corn mill, Trittiford Mill Park is now part of the Shire Country Park. This public green space now offers walking routes along the River Cole, where there is plenty of wildlife to spot. The mill pond also provides an idyllic spot for fishing.

🌐 birmingham.gov.uk/parks

Victoria Common / ©Birmingham Museums Trust

VICTORIA COMMON

Birmingham City Council
Church Road, Northfield, B31 2BB

Green Flag Award winning Victoria Common is located in the heart of Northfield town centre. It has a well balanced landscape combining open grassland, ornamental gardens and great facilities for sport and play. The Northfield Carnival is held at the common each year.

🌐 birmingham.gov.uk/parks

WARD END PARK

Birmingham City Council
Ward End Park Road, Birmingham, B8 3PH

A Green Flag Award winning park, there are two playgrounds in the park, one close to the Ward End Park Road entrance and one in the middle of the park. Ward End Park House is located within the park and dates back to 1759. There are also basketball and tennis courts within the park.

🌐 birmingham.gov.uk/parks

WITTON LAKES

Birmingham City Council
Gipsy Lane, Witton, B23 7AS

Witton Lakes boasts two lakes, open grasslands, wooded areas, and a wildflower meadow. There are also tearooms and walking trails around the lakes.

🌐 birmingham.gov.uk/parks

WOODGATE VALLEY COUNTRY PARK

Birmingham City Council
Clapgate Lane, Bartley Green, B32 3DS

Situated in 450 acres of countryside, Woodgate Valley Country Park has mixed, mature hedgerows, meadows, woodland, and small ponds. The Bourn Brook runs through the park. Over 250 species of plants have been found, with the damp meadow areas being especially rich and producing wonderful displays of wild flowers in spring and summer. The meadows also attract many kinds of butterflies and over 90 species of birds have been recorded in the park. The park is also home to Hole Farm Trekking Centre, where children and adults can go pony trekking and learn to ride, and Woodgate Valley Urban Farm.

🌐 birmingham.gov.uk/parks

Woodgate Valley Country Park / ©Birmingham Museums Trust

ACOCKS GREEN LIBRARY
Birmingham City Council
Shirley Road, Acocks Green, B27 7XH

🌐 birmingham.gov.uk/libraries
✉ acocks.green.library@birmingham.gov.uk

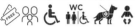

ASTON LIBRARY
Birmingham City Council
99 Whitehead Road, Aston, B6 6EJ

🌐 birmingham.gov.uk/libraries
✉ aston.library@birmingham.gov.uk

BALSALL HEATH LIBRARY
Birmingham City Council
Moseley Road, Balsall Heath, B12 9BX

🌐 birmingham.gov.uk/libraries
✉ balsall.heath.library@birmingham.gov.uk

BARTLEY GREEN LIBRARY
Birmingham City Council
Adams Hill, Barley Green, B32 3QG

🌐 birmingham.gov.uk/libraries
✉ bartley.green.library@birmingham.gov.uk

BIRCHFIELD LIBRARY
Birmingham City Council
Trinity Road, Aston, B6 6AH

🌐 birmingham.gov.uk/libraries
✉ birchfield.library@birmingham.gov.uk

BLOOMSBURY LIBRARY AT THE POD
Birmingham City Council
Oliver Street, Birmingham, B7 4NX

🌐 birmingham.gov.uk/libraries
✉ bloomsbury.library@birmingham.gov.uk

BOLDMERE LIBRARY
Birmingham City Council
119 Boldmere Road, Sutton Coldfield, B73 5TU

🌐 birmingham.gov.uk/libraries
✉ boldmere.library@birmingham.gov.uk

CASTLE VALE LIBRARY
Birmingham City Council
Spitfire House, 10 High Street, Castle Vale, B35 7PR

🌐 birmingham.gov.uk/libraries
✉ castle.vale.library@birmingham.gov.uk

DRUIDS HEATH LIBRARY
Birmingham City Council
Idmiston Croft, Druid's Heath, B14 5NJ

🌐 birmingham.gov.uk/libraries
✉ druids.heath.library@birmingham.gov.uk

ERDINGTON LIBRARY
Birmingham City Council
Orphanage Road, Erdington, B24 9HP

🌐 birmingham.gov.uk/libraries
✉ erdington.library@birmingham.gov.uk

FRANKLEY LIBRARY

Birmingham City Council
Balaam Wood Academy, Frankley, B45 0EU

🌐 birmingham.gov.uk/libraries
✉ frankley.library@birmingham.gov.uk

GLEBE FARM LIBRARY

Birmingham City Council
Glebe Farm Road, Stechford, B33 9NA

🌐 birmingham.gov.uk/libraries
✉ glebe.farm.library@birmingham.gov.uk

HALL GREEN LIBRARY

Birmingham City Council
1221 Stratford Road, Hall Green, B28 9AD

🌐 birmingham.gov.uk/libraries
✉ hall.green.library@birmingham.gov.uk

HANDSWORTH LIBRARY

Birmingham City Council
Soho Road, Handsworth, B21 9DP

🌐 birmingham.gov.uk/libraries
✉ handsworth.library@birmingham.gov.uk

HARBORNE LIBRARY

Birmingham City Council
High Street, Harborne, B17 9QG

🌐 birmingham.gov.uk/libraries
✉ harborne.library@birmingham.gov.uk

KINGS HEATH LIBRARY

Birmingham City Council
High Street, Kings Heath, B14 7SW

🌐 birmingham.gov.uk/libraries
✉ kings.heath.library@birmingham.gov.uk

KINGS NORTON LIBRARY

Birmingham City Council
Pershore Road South, Kings Norton, B30 3EU

🌐 birmingham.gov.uk/libraries
✉ kings.norton.library@birmingham.gov.uk

KINGSTANDING LIBRARY

Birmingham City Council
Kingstanding Road, Kingstanding, B44 9ST

🌐 birmingham.gov.uk/libraries
✉ kingstanding.library@birmingham.gov.uk

Library of Birmingham / ©Library of Birmingham

LIBRARY OF BIRMINGHAM
Birmingham City Council
Centenary Square, Broad Street, Birmingham, B1 2ND

Situated in Centenary Square, next to the REP, the Library of Birmingham provides a showcase for Birmingham's internationally important collections of archives, photography and rare books. Facilities include a state-of-the-art gallery space, opening up public access to the collections. It is also home to the BFI Mediatheque, providing free access to the National Film Archive. Other facilities include a flexible studio theatre, an outdoor amphitheatre and stunning views of the city from the the roof terraces on levels 3 and 7. The library offers a full range of children's activities including Rhymetime and Story Time along with dedicated spaces for children and teenagers. The library also offers visitor membership, book

Library of Birmingham / ©Birmingham City council

browsing and free internet access along with access to free resources that support learning in a range of formats. There are study spaces for children, young people and adults. The Library Shop and Tourist Information are located on the ground floor.

🌐 birmingham.gov.uk/libraries
✉ enquiries@libraryofbirmingham.com

MERE GREEN LIBRARY

Birmingham City Council
30A Mere Green Road, Sutton Coldfield, B75 5BT

🌐 birmingham.gov.uk/libraries
✉ mere.green.library@birmingham.gov.uk

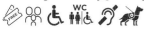

NORTHFIELD LIBRARY

Birmingham City Council
77 Church Road, Northfield, B31 2LB

🌐 birmingham.gov.uk/libraries
✉ northfield.library@birmingham.gov.uk

PERRY COMMON LIBRARY

Birmingham City Council
College Road, Perry Common, B44 0HH

🌐 birmingham.gov.uk/libraries
✉ perry.common.library@birmingham.gov.uk

QUINTON LIBRARY

Birmingham City Council
Ridgacre Road, Quinton, B32 2TW

🌐 birmingham.gov.uk/libraries
✉ quinton.library@birmingham.gov.uk

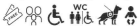

SELLY OAK LIBRARY

Birmingham City Council
Touchbase Pears, Bristol Road, Selly Oak, B29 6NA

🌐 birmingham.gov.uk/libraries
✉ selly.oak.library@birmingham.gov.uk

SHARD END LIBRARY

Birmingham City Council
All Saints Square, Shard End Crescent, B34 7AG

🌐 birmingham.gov.uk/libraries
✉ shard.end.library@birmingham.gov.uk

SHELDON LIBRARY

Birmingham City Council
Brays Road, Sheldon, B26 2RJ

🌐 birmingham.gov.uk/libraries
✉ sheldon.library@birmingham.gov.uk

SMALL HEATH LIBRARY

Birmingham City Council
Muntz Street, Small Heath, B10 9RX

🌐 birmingham.gov.uk/libraries
✉ small.heath.library@birmingham.gov.uk

SOUTH YARDLEY LIBRARY

Birmingham City Council
Yardley Road, Yardley, B25 8LT

🌐 birmingham.gov.uk/libraries
✉ south.yardley.library@birmingham.gov.uk

SPARKHILL LIBRARY

Birmingham City Council
641 Stratford Road, Sparkhill, B11 4EA

🌐 birmingham.gov.uk/libraries
✉ sparkhill.library@birmingham.gov.uk

SPRING HILL LIBRARY

Birmingham City Council
Spring Hill, Birmingham, B18 7BH

🌐 birmingham.gov.uk/libraries
✉ spring.hill.library@birmingham.gov.uk

STIRCHLEY LIBRARY

Birmingham City Council
Bournville Lane, Stirchley, B30 2JT

🌐 birmingham.gov.uk/libraries
✉ stirchley.library@birmingham.gov.uk

SUTTON COLDFIELD LIBRARY

Birmingham City Council
Lower Parade, Sutton Coldfield, B72 1XX

🌐 birmingham.gov.uk/libraries
✉ sutton.coldfield.library@birmingham.gov.uk

TOWER HILL LIBRARY

Birmingham City Council
Tower Hill, Perry Barr, B42 1LG

🌐 birmingham.gov.uk/libraries
✉ tower.hill.library@birmingham.gov.uk

WALMLEY LIBRARY

Birmingham City Council
Walmley Road, Sutton Coldfield, B76 1NP

🌐 birmingham.gov.uk/libraries
✉ walmley.library@birmingham.gov.uk

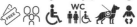

WARD END LIBRARY

Birmingham City Council
Washwood Heath Road, Ward End, B8 2HF

🌐 birmingham.gov.uk/libraries
✉ ward.end.library@birmingham.gov.uk

WEOLEY CASTLE LIBRARY

Birmingham City Council
76 Beckbury Road, Weoley, B29 5HR

🌐 birmingham.gov.uk/libraries
✉ weoley.castle.library@birmingham.gov.uk

YARDLEY WOOD LIBRARY

Birmingham City Council
Highfield Road, Birmingham, B14 4DU

🌐 birmingham.gov.uk/libraries
✉ yardley.wood.library@birmingham.gov.uk

COVENTRY

St Marys Guildhall / ©Coventry City Council

Bagot's Castle / ©Bagot's Castle

BAGOT'S CASTLE

Church Road, Baginton, CV8 3AR

Bagot's Castle is the ruins of a 14th-century castle in a picturesque setting with educational visitor centre, summer house and picnic area. There is also a children's trail and woodland walks, ornamental ponds and a Second World War tank testing area.

🌐 bagotscastle.org.uk
✉ delia@bagotscastle.org.uk

THE CHARTERHOUSE

Historic Coventry Trust
London Road, Coventry, CV1 2JB

Opening to the public for the first time after restoration by Historic Coventry Trust, visit the Charterhouse, one of only nine Carthusian monasteries built in Britain. Visitors can experience this Grade I Listed 14th-century building with its fine wall paintings, panelled rooms and tranquil walled gardens. Find out the story of this fascinating building and its residents and keep a look out for a wide range of family activities and events.

🌐 historiccoventry.org.uk
✉ admin@historiccoventry.org.uk

The Charterhouse / ©Historic Coventry Trust

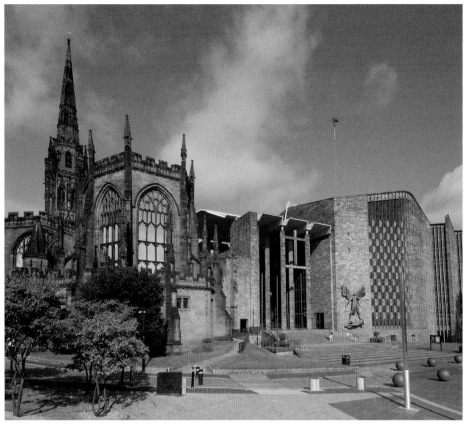

Coventry Cathedral / ©Coventry Cathedral

COVENTRY CATHEDRAL

Priory Street, Coventry, CV1 5FB

The Cathedral Church of St Michael, commonly known as Coventry Cathedral, is the seat of the Bishop of Coventry and the Diocese of Coventry within the Church of England. As soon as it was opened in 1962, the cathedral became a major attraction, welcoming thousands of visitors each year. Tourists and pilgrims come from all over the world to experience this extraordinary building and to share something of the quest for peace and reconciliation embodied by the dramatic contrast of the ruin, destroyed during the Coventry blitz in the Second World War, and the new cathedral, which was built adjacent. While visiting the cathedral, visitors can also climb 180 steps to the top of the cathedral tower and take in magnificent views of Coventry!

🌐 coventrycathedral.org.uk
✉ visits@coventrycathedral.org.uk

The Coventry Music Museum / ©Coventry Music Museum

THE COVENTRY MUSIC MUSEUM
110 Richmond Street, Coventry, CV2 4ED

The Coventry Music Museum celebrates all types of music that have hailed from the region, from Delia Derbyshire, King and Hazel O'Connor through to The Specials, Selecter, Panjabi MC and the Enemy, and so many more. Visitors can sit in the car that featured in the video for the song "*Ghost Town*", the Specials last chart topper, and vote for their favourite record. The museum is also part of the 2-Tone Village where you will find shops, a cafe, the Coventry Music Wall of Hits and the Reggae Stars Wall.

🌐 covmm.co.uk
✉️ Godivarocks@Yahoo.co.uk

COVENTRY TRANSPORT MUSEUM
Millennium Place, Coventry, CV1 1JD

Coventry Transport Museum houses the largest publicly owned collection of British vehicles and tells the story of a city which changed the world through transport. Visitors can expect captivating displays, interactive galleries, and highly immersive exhibitions. The 14 fully accessible galleries are home to the fastest vehicle in the world, pioneering bicycles, transport champions and many of the most innovative, memorable and luxurious vehicles of the last 200 years.

🌐 transport-museum.com
✉️ info@culturecoventry.com

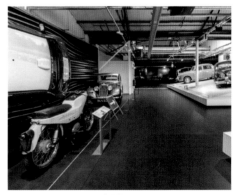

Coventry Transport Museum / ©Garry Jones

Coventry Watch Museum / ©Coventry Watch Museum

COVENTRY WATCH MUSEUM

Court 7, Rear of Samoan Joes Tikki Bar (formerly The Shakespeare), Spon Street, Coventry, CV1 3BA

Discover Coventry's unique clock and watchmaking heritage, and how the craftspeople in these industries and their families lived. The site is the remaining part of a Coventry court and is probably the last example of what was a common dwelling situation in the city in the 18th- and 19th-centuries. While renovations take place, a temporary museum has been set up using the ground floor of the existing buildings, a temporary space and also a building that was used as an air raid shelter during the Second World War by Rotherham & Sons Clock & Watch manufacturers of Coventry.

🌐 coventrywatchmuseum.co.uk
✉ coventrywatchmuseum@gmail.com

HERBERT ART GALLERY & MUSEUM

Jordan Well, Coventry, CV1 5QP

Located in the historic centre of Coventry, next to the ruins of the cathedral, the Herbert Art Gallery & Museum is the perfect place to

Herbert Art Gallery & Museum / ©Garry Jones

delve into city's history and engage with art and culture. Investigate the natural world, modern art, and Old Masters. Wander through dazzling interactive displays and enjoy the latest exhibitions while admiring the building's unique architecture. As well as the art gallery's ever-changing displays which are often created in partnership with national museums, the Herbert offers a wide range of talks, fantastic events and inventive workshops for adults and families. Also home to the Coventry Archives, the Herbert is the city's destination for historical documents, photographs, maps and archival material.

🌐 theherbert.org
✉ info@culturecoventry.com

LONDON ROAD CEMETERY: PAXTON'S ARBORETUM

Coventry City Council & Historic Coventry Trust
London Road, Coventry, CV1 2JT

This 19th-century cemetery and arboretum was created by the famous landscape designer Joseph Paxton as a park and public burial ground and is filled with native and exotic trees. Open every day to the public, you can enjoy the unique landscape, explore themed trails to 'meet the residents' or find out about the remarkable collection of specimen trees. Visit

Historic Coventry Trust's website to find out about the variety of activities and special events on offer.

🌐 historiccoventry.org.uk
✉ admin@historiccoventry.org.uk

LUNT ROMAN FORT

Coventry Road, Baginton, CV8 3AJ

Explore the history of Roman Britain in this partially reconstructed fort. Visit the exhibition in the granary, a traditional Roman food and weapon store, and imagine yourself training horses in the gyrus – a feature not found inside a Roman fort anywhere else. The fort also features ramparts where visitors can discover how the Romans would have defended it. With children's activity trails, demonstrations and event days during the school holidays, there is lots to see and do for all ages.

🌐 luntromanfort.org
✉ info@culturecoventry.com

St Mary's Guildhall / ©Coventry City Council

ST MARY'S GUILDHALL

Bayley Lane, Coventry, CV1 5RN

Located in the city's historic Cathedral Quarter, the magnificent medieval interiors and fine artworks of the Guildhall offer a window into Coventry's glorious past, a fascinating experience in the very heart of the city. Join Mary, Queen of Scots, and Shakespeare on the long list of visitors to have passed through the doors of this historic building.

🌐 stmarysguildhall.co.uk

✉ guildhall@coventry.gov.uk

THE WEAVER'S HOUSE

121 Upper Spon Street, Spon End, Coventry, CV1 3BQ

Situated in Spon Street, one of the most historic areas in Coventry, a terrace of six cottages built in 1455 has been brought back to life as a living museum. One of the cottages has been restored to show how it would have looked in 1540 and how John Croke, a Coventry narrow-loom weaver and his family would have lived and worked. At the back of the Weaver's House is a medieval garden showing the plants that would have been grown for food, flavouring, medicine and household use. The house is open to visitors on various dates throughout the year, prebooking is advised.

🌐 theweavershouse.org

✉ info@theweavershouse.org

Weavers House / ©Claire Chamberlain

Coventry Canal Basin / ©Canal & River Trust

THE BALLROOM CLIMBING WALL

Ironmonger Row, Coventry, CV1 1LZ

Coventry's first dedicated climbing centre, the Ballroom Climbing Wall offers a colourful, geometric design and a dedicated kids zone painted with jungle beasties which offers a less challenging ascent. The team welcome climbers of any ability – from beginners to experts – and offers instructor led session.

🌐 ballroomclimbing.co.uk

✉ team@ballroomclimbing.co.uk

COVENTRY CANAL BASIN

Canal & River Trust

Coventry Canal Basin, Coventry, CV1 4LY

Coventry Canal Basin is where the 38 miles of the Coventry Canal start. The basin has witnessed many fascinating changes over the years. It used to serve as an important industrial hub for the North Warwickshire collieries. Goods were loaded and unloaded here and then bound towards the Midlands via the Trent & Mersey Canal, or the Oxford Canal towards London. Today, no longer filled with the hustle and bustle of the industrial era, the basin is a place where you can relax, go for a stroll, or have a drink and enjoy a view of the remnants of the past such as the historic Draper's Field Bridge. The basin is also where the 5½ mile green corridor starts, leading along the towpath to Hawkesbury Junction – this canal stretch is perfect for walking, cycling and enjoying the local nature.

🌐 canalrivertrust.org.uk/places-to-visit/
coventry-canal-basin

✉ enquiries.westmidlands@canalrivertrust.org.uk

Fargo Village / ©Ian Bradley

FARGO VILLAGE

Far Gosford Street, Coventry, CV1 5EA

A creative arts village with 40+ independent creative businesses, as well as two venues that can be used for a variety of events including performing arts, music, conferences, and much more. The village is also home to Sgt. Bilko's Vintage Emporium and the Phil Silvers Archival Museum.

🌐 fargovillage.co.uk

✉ fargo@fargovillage.co.uk

PLANET ICE COVENTRY

Croft Road, Coventry, CV1 3AZ

Planet Ice is Europe's Number 1 for Ice Leisure. In addition to all the ice related sports and leisure programmes run at Planet Ice Coventry

such as Skate Excellence and Hockey Excellence courses, the arenas also host various concerts, shows and alternative sporting events.

🌐 planet-ice.co.uk

✉ boxoffice@planet-ice.co.uk

Planet Ice / ©Planet Ice / Coventry Telegraph

RICOH ARENA
Judds Lane, Longford, Coventry, CV6 6AQ

Since opening in 2005, Ricoh Arena has become a world-class destination for sport and entertainment. Home to Wasps Rugby, the main stadium can accommodate more than 32,000 spectators, and has played host to major international sporting events and to some of the worlds biggest music and entertainment acts.

🌐 ricoharena.com

✉ info@ricoharena.com

Sgt. Bilko's Vintage Emporium / ©The British Phil Silvers Appreciation Society and the Phil Silvers Archival Museum

SGT BILKO'S VINTAGE EMPORIUM AND THE PHIL SILVERS ARCHIVAL MUSEUM
FarGo Village, Far Gosford Street, Coventry, CV1 5ED

Sgt Bilko's Vintage Emporium is a unique venture situated in FarGo Village specialising in vintage and modern film and television memorabilia. With a strong emphasis of everything 'cult' the store caters for a wide range of tastes, offering a varied selection of collectables. The Emporium is also home to The

Phil Silvers Archival Museum, dedicated to the life and work of actor and comedian Phil Silvers. It is Coventry's smallest museum - and in all likelihood one of the smallest in the world - but the Phil Silvers Archival Museum is a sight to behold

🌐 bpsas.co.uk

✉ steviebilko@aol.com

THE WAVE WATERPARK
New Union Street, Coventry, CV1 2PS

Making a splash in the heart of Coventry, the Wave has something for everyone with the thrills of six high-octane slides that are precision-engineered to fill you with excitement, a state-of-the-art health and fitness suite to get the blood pumping and a wave pool. The Wave also boasts a relaxing cafe, lazy river and a luxurious Mana Spa for those who just want to kick back and let their troubles float away.

🌐 thewavecoventry.com

✉ wavereception@cvlife.co.uk

The Wave Waterpark / ©Mark Radford Photography

The Albany Theatre / ©The Albany Theatre

THE ALBANY THEATRE

Albany Road, Coventry, CV5 6JQ

The Albany is a beautiful Art Deco theatre in the heart of Coventry staging in-house and professional touring dance, drama, music and comedy productions.

🌐 albanytheatre.co.uk

✉ info@albanytheatre.co.uk

THE ARCHES

22 - 23 Arches Industrial Estate, Coventry CV1 3JQ

Situated in Spon End, the Arches is a live music venue hosting local talent and touring bands including some tribute acts.

🌐 facebook.com/archesvenuecoventry

✉ archesvenuecoventry@gmail.com

Belgrade Theatre / ©Belgrade Theatre

BELGRADE THEATRE

Belgrade Square, Coventry, West Midlands, CV1 1GS

Coventry's largest professional theatre, the Belgrade offers an exciting mix of entertaining and engaging live experiences all under one roof, aiming to entertain, inspire and unleash creativity in Coventry and beyond.

🌐 belgrade.co.uk

✉ boxoffice@belgrade.co.uk

ODEON COVENTRY

Skydome, Croft Road, CV1 3AZ

Situated on outskirts of the city centre, ODEON Coventry features nine screens showing the latest film releases for all ages. Visitors can also experience the magic of cinema in RealD 3D.

🌐 odeon.co.uk

CRITERION THEATRE

Berkeley Road South, Earlsdon, CV5 6EF

Situated in the heart of Earlsdon, the Criterion Theatre is an experienced repetory theatre company that produces about seven productions annually.

🌐 criteriontheatre.co.uk

✉ boxoffice@criteriontheatre.co.uk

Criterion Theatre / ©Criterion Theatre

Theatre Absolute / ©Andrew Moore

THEATRE ABSOLUTE/ SHOP FRONT THEATRE

Shop Front Theatre, 38 City Arcade, Coventry, CV1 3HW

Inspired by Chicago's store front theatre scene, this once fish and chip shop provides a dynamic yet intimate performance space for the Theatre Absolute theatre company.

🌐 theatreabsolute.co.uk

✉ info@theatreabsolute.co.uk

SHOWCASE CINEMA DE LUX COVENTRY

Gielgud Way, Walsgrave, CV2 2SZ

Experience the magic of the movies at Showcase Cinema de Lux, with 14 screens, all with fully customisable recliner seating showing the latest blockbuster releases and Event Cinema performances. This state-of-the-art cinema also features a lounge bar. in the lobby selling hot and cold food and a full range of alcoholic and soft drinks. The XPlus auditorium gives the ultimate cinema experience with a supersized, giant screen and immersive Dolby Atmos sound. Also includes a full Costa Coffee store.

🌐 showcasecinemas.co.uk

THE TIN MUSIC AND ARTS

Units 1 - 4, The Canal Basin, CV1 4LY

The unique and intimate setting for a music venue, The Tin at The Coal Vaults, makes for a truly stand-alone and incomparable place for any event. The 18th-century space, set in the Coventry Canal Basin's former coal storage building, oozes character with its exposed brick walls and curved ceilings. The venue is set across two vaults, one side with bar and raised area, the other with stage and dance floor.

🌐 thetinmusicandarts.org.uk

The Tin Music and Arts / ©Tin Music and Arts

COVENTRY PARKS, GARDENS AND NATURE RESERVES

ALLESLEY PARK

Coventry City Council
Allesley Hall Drive, Allesley Park, Coventry, CV5 9AD

A Green Flag Award winning park, this picturesque historic park dating back to the 12th-century provides acres of green space for the whole family to enjoy. Tarmac paths provide access for all through the park's rolling landscape with established parkland trees interspersed with views towards Allesley village and its church. The Georgian walled garden is an interesting and attractive feature in the park and children especially enjoy visiting the large playground, including one of the tallest space-nets available. A 'pop-up' cafe provides drinks and light refreshments for visitors during busy periods and a crazy golf course and a 'pitch and putt' golf course are also popular with equipment including golf-clubs available to hire from the park office. Families with children can also enjoy a visit to the 'fairy garden' and everyone can enjoy picnics on the extensive grassed areas or a kick-about on the informal football pitch.

- coventry.gov.uk/allesleypark
- allesleyparksoffice@coventry.gov.uk

Allesley Park / ©Coventry City Council

Caludon Castle Park / ©Coventry City Council

BRANDON MARSH NATURE RESERVE

Warwickshire Wildlife Trust
Brandon Lane, Coventry, CV3 3GW

Brandon Marsh Nature Reserve covers 220 acres and features a wide variety of large pools, bird hides, woodland walks and wildflower meadows. This former quarry has been transformed into a European Site of Special Scientific Interest and is home to a number of iconic species including kingfisher, cuckoos and otter. The reserve is also frequented by visiting osprey, pied flycatcher and other rare migratory species. The visitor centre is a great place to start your visit, and includes a tearoom and gift shop. The accessible network of paths and boardwalks allow visitors to explore pools, reedbeds and woodlands and get closer to nature.

- warwickshirewildlifetrust.org.uk/BrandonMarsh
- enquiries@wkwt.org.uk

CALUDON CASTLE PARK
Coventry City Council
Farren Road, Coventry CV2 5EH

A Green Flag Award winning park, Caludon Castle Park is located three miles east of Coventry city centre and it is the area park for the south of the city. Although smaller in size than other area parks, it offers a valued green space experience for local people. The site contains two Scheduled Ancient Monuments and the remains of Caludon Castle which is Grade I Listed. The park is informally divided into zones including sport and play to the east and the historical features to the west and north. The park also features multi-use sports pitches, walking trails, an outdoor gym and a medieval themed children's playground.

🌐 coventry.gov.uk/caludoncastlepark

COOMBE ABBEY PARK
Coventry City Council
Brinklow Road, Binley, Coventry, CV3 2AB

A Green Flag award winning park, Coombe Abbey Park is ideal for a family day out, or a quiet little picnic. The Park offers visitors 500 acres of beautiful gardens, woodland, lakeside walks, and parkland. The diverse Capability Brown, Nesfield and Miller landscapes make it ideal for everyone, from families to wildlife enthusiasts and those just looking for a quiet stroll in the woodland there is always something to see and do. Throughout the year a number of events and activities take place in and around the park – see website for details. The grounds host a well-stocked fishery, two children's play areas, bird hide, orienteering course, Go Ape course and is also home to the 4 star Coombe Abbey Hotel who operate three catering outlets

within the park grounds Café in the Park, Kiosk in the Park and an ice-cream parlour.

🌐 coventry.gov.uk/coombe
✉ Coombe@coventry.gov.uk

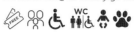

Coombe Abbey Park / ©Coventry City Council

COUNDON HALL PARK
Coventry City Council
Waste Lane, Coundon, Coventry, CV6 2EH

A large park with a range of different landscapes, the park contains a mixture of small woodlands, several large ponds and extensive areas of conservation and amenity grassland, some of which is taken up by sports pitches. A large play area is popular with children of all ages and a hard-surfaced path provides access along much of the perimeter of the park. The park is also the home of the Normandy Day Peace Orchard which pays tribute to those who took part in the D-Day landings in the Second World War.

🌐 coventry.gov.uk/parklocations

Longford Park / ©Coventry City Council

LONGFORD PARK

Coventry City Council
Longford Road, Longford, Coventry, CV6 6DW

The largest of the Coventry's area parks, Longford Park serves the community in the north of the city. It is a well-established green space with expanses of grass, colourful bedding schemes, picturesque tree lined river walk, ecological and wildlife areas and a range of facilities for all the family to enjoy. The extensive and well used footpath system is ideal as an exercise facility using the distance marked routes (Magic Mile Walking Route), and as a dog walking venue. The park holds a Green Flag Award and boasts facilities such as an enclosed children's play area, floodlit multi-use games area, artificial cricket wicket for informal use, an orienteering course, skate park, and outdoor gym. The parks is also host to community events including the annual Bands in the Park concerts in the summer, and has an active friends of group.

🌐 coventry.gov.uk/longfordpark

NAULS MILL PARK

Coventry City Council
Coundon Road, Coundon, Coventry, CV1 4AR

Nauls Mill Park is a historic park dating back to 1908. Despite being close to the city centre, this hidden gem provides areas of tranquil green space surrounded by mature trees with flowerbeds and a large ornamental pond. Facilities include a children's play area whilst after a short walk through the park, two fenced ball games areas provide opportunities for 5-a-side football, basketball and other sports. The park also plays host to occasional band concerts in the summer.

🌐 coventry.gov.uk/parklocations

PARKWOOD MEADOWS

Coventry City Council
Parkwood Lane, Canley, Coventry, CV4 8AY

Parkwood Meadows opened in 2009 offering a completely natural play experience. Children and young people can explore, climb, run and discover nature in a visionary design that complements the ancient woodland nearby.

🌐 coventry.gov.uk/parklocations

SWANSWELL PARK AND POOL

Coventry City Council
Stoney Stanton Road, Coventry, CV1 4FF

This popular green space is right next to the city centre and is a popular route into and out of town for students and other residents living nearby. The ornamental pool in the park has been here since the 12th-century and was probably first created as a medieval monastic fish pond. The pool is still popular with local anglers and is home to all sorts of waterfowl including swans, ducks, geese, moorhens, coots and others. The park occasionally hosts Bands in the Parks concerts in the summer and was recently refurbished to provide play equipment for younger children and the very latest in outdoor exercise equipment for older visitors.

🌐 coventry.gov.uk/parklocations

WAR MEMORIAL PARK

Coventry City Council
Kenilworth Road, Coventry, CV3 6PT

The War Memorial Park is Coventry's premier park and attracts around 400,000 visitors annually from all over the city, and beyond. Many come to enjoy a casual visit, while others come to take part in some of the many special events that take place throughout the year. Roughly 120 acres in size, the park is made up of two areas, firstly the formal garden with the war memorial, and secondly with playing fields, foot golf, bowling green, tennis courts, orienteering course, Splash 'n' Play park, skatepark and children's play areas. There is also a 1.6-mile circular footpath around the park. The War Memorial Park is a Grade II Listed park recognised by Historic England and the War Memorial itself is also a Grade II Listed building.

🌐 coventry.gov.uk/wmp
✉ WarMemorialPark@coventry.gov.uk

War Memorial Park / ©Coventry City Council

WYKEN SLOUGH

Coventry City Council
Aldermans Green Road, Aldermans Green, CV2 1PL

This beautiful area is a Local Nature Reserve, and forms part of the Sowe Valley Walk. Wyken Slough supports a rich variety of wildlife and is an area of natural beauty. The abundant wildlife on the site led to its designation as a Local Nature Reserve in 1991. While land drainage has greatly reduced the number of wetlands in Britain, the Slough which is made up of marshes, floodland and reedbeds has become vital for a wide range of birds, amphibians, insects and plants. The reedbeds are dominated by reed sweetgrass which provides an excellent habitat for insects such as the Brown Hawker Dragonfly. Mayflies are also a common sight at the waters edge.

🌐 coventry.gov.uk/parklocations

ALDERMOOR LIBRARY

Coventry City Council
Acorn Street, Stoke Aldermoor, CV3 1DP

🌐 coventry.gov.uk/libraries
✉ aldermoor.library@coventry.gov.uk

ALLESLEY PARK LIBRARY

Coventry City Council
Allesley Park Neighbourhood Centre, Allesley Park,
Whitaker Road, CV5 9JE

🌐 coventry.gov.uk/libraries
✉ allesleypark.library@coventry.gov.uk

BELL GREEN LIBRARY

Coventry City Council
17-23 Riley Square, Bell Green, CV2 1LS

🌐 coventry.gov.uk/libraries
✉ bellgreen.library@coventry.gov.uk

CALUDON LIBRARY

Coventry City Council
Axholme Road, Wyken, CV2 5BD

🌐 coventry.gov.uk/libraries
✉ caludon.library@coventry.gov.uk

CANLEY LIBRARY

Coventry City Council
Prior Deram Walk, Canley, CV4 8FT

🌐 coventry.gov.uk/libraries
✉ canley.library@coventry.gov.uk

Central Library / ©Coventry Library Service

CENTRAL LIBRARY

Coventry City Council
Smithford Way, Coventry, CV1 1FY

Coventry Central Library hosts a variety of in-house events for both adults and children. These include regular Rhymetime, Storytime with Crafts and Lego Storytime sessions for children and Readers Groups, Conversation Cafes, and reminiscence sessions for adults. These sessions also take place in most of Coventry's local libraries, and are also hosted as online sessions for some of these events.

🌐 coventry.gov.uk/libraries
✉ central.library@coventry.gov.uk

CHEYLESMORE LIBRARY

Cheylesmore Community Centre, Poitiers Road,
Cheylesmore, CV3 5JX

🌐 cheylesmorecentre.co.uk
✉ library@cheylesmorecentre.co.uk

COUNDON LIBRARY

Coventry City Council
Moseley Avenue, Coundon, CV6 1HT

🌐 coventry.gov.uk/libraries
✉️ coundon.library@coventry.gov.uk

EARLSDON LIBRARY

Earlsdon Avenue North, Earlsdon, CV5 6FZ

🌐 earlsdonlibrary.org.uk
✉️ admin@earlsdonlibrary.org.uk

FINHAM LIBRARY

Finham Green Road, Finham, CV3 6EP

🌐 finhamlibrary.uk
✉️ finhamlibrary@gmail.com

FOLESHILL LIBRARY

Coventry City Council
Broad Street, Foleshill, CV6 5BG

🌐 coventry.gov.uk/libraries
✉️ foleshill.library@coventry.gov.uk

HILLFIELDS LIBRARY

Coventry City Council
WATCH Centre, Victoria Street, Hillfields, CV1 5LZ

🌐 coventry.gov.uk/libraries
✉️ hillfields.library@coventry.gov.uk

HOLBROOKS LIBRARY

Holbrooks Community Care Association, The Park,
115 Holbrook Lane, Holbrooks, CV6 4DE

🌐 hccacoventry.org.uk/library
✉️ hcca@btconnect.com

JUBILEE CRESCENT LIBRARY

Coventry City Council
Jubilee Crescent Community Centre, Jubilee
Crescent, Radford, CV6 3EX

🌐 coventry.gov.uk/libraries
✉️ jubileecrescent.library@coventry.gov.uk

STOKE LIBRARY

Coventry City Council
Kingsway, Stoke, CV2 4EA

🌐 coventry.gov.uk/libraries
✉️ stoke.library@coventry.gov.uk

TILE HILL LIBRARY

Coventry City Council
Jardine Crescent, Tile Hill, CV4 9PL

🌐 coventry.gov.uk/libraries
✉️ tilehill.library@coventry.gov.uk

WILLENHALL LIBRARY

Coventry City Council
Hagard Community Centre, Remembrance Rd,
Coventry, CV3 3DG

🌐 coventry.gov.uk/libraries
✉️ willenhall.library@coventry.gov.uk

DUDLEY

Dudley Zoo & Castle / ©Dudley Zoo

Black Country Living Museum / ©Black Country Living Museum

BLACK COUNTRY LIVING MUSEUM
Tipton Road, Dudley, DY1 4SQ

An immersive experience from start to finish, Black Country Living Museum is an award-winning open air museum that tells the story of one of the very first industrialised landscapes in Britain. Set across 26 acres, visitors can explore over 40 carefully reconstructed shops, houses and industrial areas that represent the Black Country's story. Learn how steam power, human ingenuity and an increasingly interconnected world have transformed this region into a manufacturing powerhouse. Visitors can also see history brought to life before their eyes, meeting characters who can tell stories of what it was really like to live and work during this revolutionary period of history.

🌐 bclm.co.uk

✉ info@bclm.com

Dudley Museum at the Archives / ©Dudley MBC

DUDLEY MUSEUM AT THE ARCHIVES
Dudley Metropolitan Borough Council
Tipton Road, Dudley, DY1 4SQ

This modern museum tells the story of Dudley (and the wider Black Country) through time. With the galleries arranged as a timeline, visitors are given a series of snapshots of the areas amazing history. The story begins with the mining that uncovered stories of ancient worlds and follows changes to the landscape through to the artistic and tourism opportunities of today's Dudley. Visitors can sit back and watch an audio/visual telling of history and heritage of the wider Black Country and Dudley. The museum is also the headquarters to the Black Country UNESCO Global Geopark.

🌐 dudley.gov.uk/dudleymuseum

✉ museums@dudley.gov.uk

HALESOWEN ABBEY

English Heritage
Manor Way, Halesowen, B62 8RJ

Halesowen Abbey was a Premonstratensian monastery founded by Peter des Roches in 1218 with a grant of land from King John. It was an important establishment which acquired two daughter abbeys and a dependent priory in its lifetime but today only atmospheric ruins remain.

🌐 english-heritage.org.uk/visit/places/halesowen-abbey

✉ CustomerCare@English-Heritage.org.uk

HIMLEY HALL & PARK

Dudley Metropolitan Borough Council
Himley, Dudley, DY3 4DF

Himley Hall is a commanding 18th-century Palladian building set among 180 acres of Capability Brown landscaped parkland. Once the family home to the Earls of Dudley and host to royalty and high society, its coffee shop is a draw for those who use the beautiful gardens, as well as those wishing to enjoy a treat. Himley Park hosts an annual programme of outdoor events, including the famous fireworks and bonfire display, Armed Forces Day, Under 5s Day and regular Antiques Fayres.

🌐 himleyhallandpark.co.uk

✉ himley.hall@dudley.gov.uk

The Lace Guild Museum / ©The Lace Guild Museum

THE LACE GUILD MUSEUM

The Hollies, 53 Audnam, Stourbridge, DY8 4AE

The Lace Guild Museum has over 18,000 items relating to textile lace, dating from the 18th-century, including knitted, crochet and bobbin laces made across the Commonwealth. Demonstrations of all forms of lacemaking, and mini lacemaking taster workshops for children and adults are available for visitors to the museum.

🌐 laceguild.org

✉ hollies@laceguild.org

Himley Hall & Park / ©Dudley MBC

Delph Locks / ©Canal & River Trust

DELPH LOCKS

Canal & River Trust
54 Brierley Hill, DY5 2TD

Delph Locks are a series of eight narrow canal locks on the Dudley No. 1 Canal in Brierley Hill. An iron roving bridge manufactured by Horsley Ironworks stands near the top lock, while the original lock-keeper's house, built in 1779 and modified in the 19th-century, is a Grade II Listed Building, as it is one of only a few surviving houses of its type in the UK.

🌐 canalrivertrust.org.uk/places-to-visit
✉ enquiries.westmidlands@canalrivertrust.org.uk

DUDLEY CANAL AND TUNNEL TRUST

501 Birmingham New Road, Bilston, DY1 4SB

The popular 45 minute boat trips run every day from Wednesday to Sunday from 10am to 3pm, taking you deep underground into the abandoned limestone mines and tunnels under Castle Hill in Dudley. With a knowledgeable skipper providing a commentary, sound and light shows and displays this unique environment really comes alive. With a free exhibition gallery, hands-on activities and limestone trail you can explore 428 million year old limestone, journey through tunnels handmade by thousands of Black Country folk from years gone by and be amazed by the awe-inspiring caverns that the industrial revolution left behind here. It's a boat trip like no other!

🌐 dudleycanaltrust.org.uk
✉ info@dctt.org.uk

DUDLEY ZOO & CASTLE

Castle Hill, Dudley, DY1 4QF

Dudley Zoo & Castle is a 40-acre zoo located within the grounds of Dudley Castle, which opened in 1937. Home to more than 1300 animals, and has nigh on 200 species, including some of the rarest creatures on planet earth. Dudley Zoo & Castle is much more than a zoo. Hundreds of exotic and endangered animals inhabit an ancient wooded hillside, with a rich geological history, around the ruins of the 11th-century Dudley Castle and they share a site with the world's largest single collection of Modernist Tecton structures – and the country's only vintage chairlift!

🌐 dudleyzoo.org.uk
✉ admin@dudleyzoo.org.uk

Red House Class Cone / ©Dudley MBC

RED HOUSE GLASS CONE

Dudley Metropolitan Borough Council
High Street, Wordsley, Stourbridge, DY8 4AZ

Situated in Stourbridge's Glass Quarter, the Red House Glass Cone was built at the end of the 18th-century and used for the manufacture of glass until 1936 and is now one of only four glass cones left in the UK. Family-friendly events and activities take place throughout the year, including live glass blowing demonstrations and a glass fusing studio. Guided tours are available both in person or by using the Augment Reality signage on site. The gift shop and craft studios offer a range of locally produced glassware and handcrafted items. The Coffee House at the Red House Glass Cone that offers hot and cold drinks together a wide selection of homemade food and delicious cakes. The site also features several craft retailers ranging from art and jewellery to pottery and glass design.

🌐 glassquarter.dudley.gov.uk
✉ museums@dudley.gov.uk

Dudley Zoo & Castle / ©Dudley Zoo

Dudley Town Hall / ©Borough Halls

DUDLEY TOWN HALL

St James's Road, Dudley, DY1 1HP

Renowned for its superb acoustics, Dudley Town Hall possesses a wealth of history and has seen a host of famous faces pass through its doors over the years. As the largest venue in the Dudley borough this attractive venue – formerly known as Dudley Concert Hall – offers a bustling programme of world-class live entertainment including comedy, music, theatre and much more. It is also home to the popular annual Dudley Winter Ales Fayre.

🌐 boroughhalls.co.uk
✉ borough.halls@dudley.gov.uk

HALESOWEN CORNBOW HALL

10 Hagley Street, Halesowen, B63 3AT

Situated in Halesowen town centre, the Cornbow Hall is a versatile and multifunctional venue. This hidden gem provides an ideal setting for social occasions; regularly hosting a wide range of meetings and events. Adjacent to a multi-storey car park and with direct access to the venue for people with limited mobility, this well-equipped community hub offers ease of access for

everyone. The Cornbow has an ever-expanding programme of excellent live entertainment including comedy, music, theatre and wrestling.

🌐 boroughhalls.co.uk
✉ borough.halls@dudley.gov.uk

ODEON DUDLEY

Merry Hill Centre, Brierley Hill, DY5 1SY

Situated in the Merry Hill shopping centre, ODEON Dudley features 10 screens showing the latest film releases for all ages. Visitors can also experience the magic of cinema in RealD 3D.

🌐 www.odeon.co.uk

Halesowen Cornbow Hall / ©Borough Halls

SHOWCASE CINEMA DUDLEY

Castlegate Way, Dudley, DY1 4TA

Experience the magic of the movies at Showcase Dudley, with 14 screens, showing the latest blockbuster releases. This state-of-the-art cinema also features the Gallery with ultra comfortable leather sofas and access to the Gallery bar. The XPlus auditorium gives the ultimate cinema experience with a supersized, giant screen and immersive Dolby Atmos sound.

🌐 www.showcasecinemas.co.uk

STOURBRIDGE TOWN HALL

Crown Centre, Crown Lane, Stourbridge, DY8 1YE

A beautiful venue situated in the heart of Stourbridge, boasting many attractive Victorian features. Stourbridge Town Hall offers a lively programme of first-class live entertainment including comedy, music, cinema screenings, family shows and much more. A superbly equipped theatre setting, this historic venue is home to several local award-winning amateur dramatics groups, and provides a base for a broad variety of community events.

🌐 boroughhalls.co.uk

✉ borough.halls@dudley.gov.uk

Stourbridge Town Hall / ©Borough Halls

BEACON HILL AND TOWER PARK

Dudley Metropolitan Borough Council
Beacon Hill, Dudley, DY3 1NA

To the north of Sedgley Town Centre lies Beacon Hill and Beacon Tower, a Grade II Listed building. Formerly a site of intensive quarrying from 17th-century to around the time of the First World War, Beacon Hill has an industrial legacy which has created a series of parallel steep-sided ridges and gullies colonised by wildlife. The site is popular with local residents on account of the panoramic views of the industrial Black Country and contrasting Staffordshire countryside. Beacon Hill forms part of the Limestone Way with public rights of way running through Sedgley, Wren's Nest National Nature Reserve, Dudley Priory and on to Dudley Zoo and Castle.

🌐 dudley.gov.uk/things-to-do/parks-and-open-spaces/parks-in-the-borough

BUFFERY PARK AND GRAZEBROOK MEMORIAL PARK

Dudley Metropolitan Borough Council
33 Paradise, Dudley DY2 8SH

At approximately 15 acres, Green Flag Award winning Buffery Park has large areas of open flat grass, shaded and unshaded spots perfect for picnics and leisure activities, a multi-use games area, outdoor gym and a children's play area. Grazebrook Memorial Park is host to a wide variety of trees, wildflower and wildlife and located centrally within the park lies the Grazebrook First World War Memorial.

🌐 dudley.gov.uk/things-to-do/parks-and-open-spaces/parks-in-the-borough

Buffery Park / ©Dudley MBC

Bumble Hole Local Nature Reserve / ©Brenda Myers

BUMBLE HOLE AND WARRENS HALL LOCAL NATURE RESERVE

Dudley Metropolitan Borough Council
Windmill End, Dudley, DY2 9HS

A local network of nature reserves, Bumble Hole and Warrens Hall Nature Reserves are great areas for leisurely walks and picnics with open areas of grass and bustling wildlife living along the quiet canal pathways. The area is also host to the Black Country Boating Festival; an annual event held every September.

🌐 dudley.gov.uk/residents/environment/ countryside-in-dudley/nature-reserves/bumble-hole-and-warrens-hall-local-nature-reserves

COTWALL END LOCAL NATURE RESERVE

Dudley Metropolitan Borough Council
The Alley, Straits Road, Gornal Wood, Dudley, DY3 2UL

Cotwall End Valley is a Local Nature Reserve and Site of Importance for Nature Conservation, comprising a variety of habitats including rich grassland, ancient and semi-natural woodland and lowland heath. The nature reserve walk passes through picturesque wooded valleys with pools, brooks and natural springs. The site has important wildlife with nationally rare flora and fauna including several species of orchid and the endangered Great Crested Newt. The valley has a rich history and geology associated with its agricultural and industrial past. In addition to wildlife, Turner's Hill geological Site of Special Scientific Interest provides important exposures of a sequence of strata of late Silurian age, including the Sedgley Limestone and Ludlow Bone Bed.

🌐 dudley.gov.uk/things-to-do/nature-reserves/ cotwall-end-local-nature-reserve

HOMER HILL PARK

Dudley Metropolitan Borough Council
Homer Hill Road, Halesowen, B63 2UR

Positioned between Homer Hill Road and Slade Road, Homer Hill Park offers a safe, varied landscape suitable for all. The park is regularly used by families, runners, walkers, dog walkers and organised sports teams. Running through the park are managed pathways with ample resting benches. There is a secure toddler play area along with picnic benches and a wildflower and seasonal bulb section. Deeper into the park there is an open play area with natural play elements and a variety of play equipment suitable for all ages.

🌐 dudley.gov.uk/things-to-do/parks-and-open-spaces/parks-in-the-borough

HUNTINGTREE PARK

Dudley Metropolitan Borough Council
Huntingtree Road, Halesowen, B63 4HY

One of four Healthy Hubs in Dudley, Huntingtree Park is a Green Flag Award winning park. Facilities on offer include an activity centre, outdoor gym, children's play area, bowling green, tennis court and football pitch.

🌐 dudley.gov.uk/things-to-do/parks-and-open-spaces/parks-in-the-borough

KINGSWINFORD PARK (KING GEORGE VI)

Dudley Metropolitan Borough Council
Park Lane, Kingswinford, DY6 8AZ

King George VI Park is lined with trees and has a quiet family appeal. A main focal point is its pond which attracts an abundance of wildlife. The park also boasts a children's play area and

Huntingtree Park / ©Dudley MBC

The Leasowes / ©Dudley MBC

an elevated bird feeding area. The park has a raised section of trees, offsetting remarkable views of the busy park during the summer months.

🌐 dudley.gov.uk/things-to-do/parks-and-open-spaces/parks-in-the-borough

KING GEORGE V PARK

Dudley Metropolitan Borough Council
Lawnswood Road, Wordsley, Stourbridge, DY8 5BS

King George V Park in Wordsley has royal connections. Part of the park is an independent charity and registered as a King George Field, which forms part of the National memorial to his late Majesty King George V. The park has extensive recreational facilities, including tennis courts, football pitches and a children's play area, as well as large areas of flat grass, managed pathways, and beautifully maintained flower beds across its sweeping landscape.

🌐 dudley.gov.uk/things-to-do/parks-and-open-spaces/parks-in-the-borough

THE LEASOWES

Dudley Metropolitan Borough Council
Leasowes Lane, Halesowen, B62 8DH

The Leasowes is a 140-acre estate in Halesowen, comprising both house and gardens. The parkland is Grade I Listed on Historic England's Register of Parks and Gardens. Designed by the poet William Shenstone between 1743 and 1763 the site is one of the most important and influential landscapes of the 18th-century and is considered to be one of the first natural landscape gardens in England. Today, the Leasowes is of major historic significance, ranking in importance with such landscapes as Blenheim and Stowe. It is the diverse landscape of wooded valleys, open grasslands, lakes and streams created by Shenstone that makes the site so important for wildlife. The site has been managed with nature in mind since the mid-18th century and as such provides a wealth of different habitats for birds, mammals, invertebrates and locally uncommon plant species.

🌐 dudley.gov.uk/things-to-do/nature-reserves/the-leasowes

MARY STEVENS PARK

Dudley Metropolitan Borough Council
Worcester Street, Stourbridge, DY8 2AD

Green Flag Award winning Mary Stevens Park is a well-loved community asset. The park receives approximately one million visitors each year. The park is a real hive of activity year round, with daily health and fitness activities, community group events and regular heritage and wildlife activities, including Heath Pool which is popular for feeding ducks. The park facilities include an outdoor gym, a large play area, a cafe in the tea gardens, tennis courts, crown green bowls and croquet (charges apply). The park features a bandstand and is also the location of Stourbridge War Memorial.

🌐 dudley.gov.uk/things-to-do/parks-and-open-spaces/parks-in-the-borough

MILKING BANK PARK

Dudley Metropolitan Borough Council
Milking Bank, Dudley, DY1 2TP

Milking Bank Park has a wide selection of managed tarmac paths that lead down to a lovely large pond; home to an abundance of wildlife, birds and fantastic bullrushes. The park has many areas of open grass idea for team games. Running alongside are smaller grassed areas, ideal for family days out, recreation games as well as privacy for picnics. The park has flowing, hilly nature that is neither too steep or flat, making walking and running perfect activities, and features a large children's play area and sports pitches.

🌐 dudley.gov.uk/things-to-do/parks-and-open-spaces/parks-in-the-borough

Mary Stevens Park / ©Dudley MBC

Priory Park / ©Dudley MBC

NETHERTON PARK

Dudley Metropolitan Borough Council
Arch Hill Street, Netherton, DY2 9QF

With large open grass areas, ideal for team games, and smaller shaded and unshaded areas perfect for picnics and leisure activities Netherton Park has something for everyone. Netherton Park is part of the Healthy Towns project and provides parks activities through its "Healthy Hub". It hosts a selection of pathways, making the park an ideal space for walking and running. Facilities include children's play area, wildlife area links to canal and railway walks.

🌐 dudley.gov.uk/things-to-do/parks-and-open-spaces/parks-in-the-borough

PRIORY PARK

Dudley Metropolitan Borough Council
Pagnal Drive, Dudley, DY1 4EU

Located a short walk from Dudley town centre, Priory Park retains most of its original features from opening in the 1930s including a statue of local Wimbledon Champion, Dorothy Round. Facilities include the Community Café at the Pavilion which features plaques to commemorate famed local footballer, Duncan Edwards, sports pitches and courts, a sunken pond and children's play area. The historic ruins are a Scheduled Ancient Monument.

🌐 dudley.gov.uk/things-to-do/parks-and-open-spaces/parks-in-the-borough

Saltwells Nature Reserve / ©Martin Weaver

SALTWELLS NATIONAL NATURE RESERVE

Dudley Metropolitan Borough Council
Saltwells Lane, Dudley, DY2 0AP

A mixture of world-class geology, bluebell covered ancient woodland and nationally important heritage, Saltwells National Nature Reserve is now one of the UK's largest urban nature reserves, covering 247 acres. Features of the reserve include Daphne Pool – home to 16 recorded species of dragonfly and an extensive bluebell woodland with woodland birds. It is also a geological Site of Special Scientific Interest – showing the best exposure of the Staffordshire coalfields and Brewin's Cutting, a significant site in the Black Country Geo Park.

🌐 dudley.gov.uk/resident/environment/ countryside/nature-reserves/saltwells-local-nature-reserve-/

✉ Saltwells.Country@dudley.gov. uk

SEDGLEY HALL FARM PARK

Dudley Metropolitan Borough Council
Northway, Dudley, DY3 3RE

Sedgley Hall Farm Park is unique in character compared to Dudley's other parks. Situated upon the urban fringe, this former farmland includes sweeping landscapes with areas of heathland, streams, and ponds. At 17 acres in size the park is located close to the Shropshire borders. The top of the park displays extensive spectacular views for miles into the Shropshire countryside. The diverse landscape terrain makes this area ideal for cross country physical activities such as running and orienteering.

🌐 dudley.gov.uk/things-to-do/parks-and-open-spaces/parks-in-the-borough

SILVER JUBILEE PARK

Dudley Metropolitan Borough Council
Off Birmingham New Road, Coseley, WV14 9SZ

Located close to Coseley railway station, Green Flag Award winning Silver Jubilee Park is part of the Healthy Towns project and has an outdoor gym and activity centre. There is also a children's play area, walking trails and a variety of sports pitches. Running along the perimeter of the park are trees providing a home to an abundance of wildlife and birds.

⊕ dudley.gov.uk/things-to-do/parks-and-open-spaces/parks-in-the-borough

STEVEN'S PARK

Dudley Metropolitan Borough Council
Thorns Road , Stourbridge, DY5 2HP

Steven's Park offers extensive recreational facilities and many areas of managed grass across its sweeping landscape. The park hosts spectacular views to surrounding areas and catches the stunning setting sun just perfectly At approximately 17 acres the park has large areas of open flat grass, with smaller shaded and unshaded areas perfect for picnics and leisure activities. One of these large areas is utilised as a football pitch, by a variety of teams.

There is also a children's play area, skate park, and a bandstand.

⊕ dudley.gov.uk/things-to-do/parks-and-open-spaces/parks-in-the-borough

STEVEN'S PARK, WOLLESCOTE

Dudley Metropolitan Borough Council
Wollescote Road, Stourbridge, Dudley, DY9 7JG

At 67 acres Steven's Park offers extensive recreational facilities and beautifully managed flower beds and grassed areas. In the heart of the park lies Wollescote Hall, a Grade II Listed building steeped in local history. This park hosts spectacular views to surrounding countryside and back towards the Black Country. Facilities include a children's play area and picnic benches, tennis courts and both crown and flat green bowls. In the lower section of the park is Ludgbridge Brook which has tree line of mature willows and alders, this area is a haven for numerous types of wildlife. In addition, there is a large area of playing field, which is maintained as a cricket pitch, a sensory garden and a historic walled garden.

⊕ dudley.gov.uk/things-to-do/parks-and-open-spaces/parks-in-the-borough

Steven's Park, Wollescote / ©Dudley MBC

WALL HEALTH PARK

Dudley Metropolitan Borough Council
Albion street, Wall Heath, Kingswinford, DY6 0JP

Located along quiet roads the park offers open, flowing grassed landscapes ideal for picnics, family days out, team games and health activities such as walking and running. A path runs into the park directly to the children's play area, and along the path are suitably positioned benches. The open grassed area is surrounded by a wide selection of trees, including some picturesque pines.

🌐 dudley.gov.uk/things-to-do/parks-and-open-spaces/parks-in-the-borough

WREN'S NEST NATIONAL NATURE RESERVE

Dudley Metropolitan Borough Council
Wren's Hill Road, Dudley, DY1 3SB

Wren's Nest National Nature Reserve is of exceptional importance. As the most important site of the Black Country Geo Park, it is one of the most notable geological locations in the UK and is visited and studied by geologists from all over the world. Over 400 million years ago, the area where Dudley now stands was covered by coral reefs and tropical seas providing an environment for the famous fossils found there today. Over 700 types of fossil are known to have come from Wren's Nest, 186 of which were first discovered and described here and 86 are found nowhere else on earth. The reserve is also a winner of a Green Flag Award.

🌐 dudley.gov.uk/things-to-do/nature-reserves/wrens-nest-national-nature-reserve

Wren's Nest Nature Reserve / ©Dudley MBC

Archives and Local History Centre / © Greenwich Leisure Ltd.

ARCHIVES AND LOCAL HISTORY CENTRE

Dudley Metropolitan Borough Council/ Better (GLL)

Tipton Road, Dudley, DY1 4SQ

The Dudley Archives and Local History Centre allows you to explore the wonderful heritage preserved there. The collections include a Papal Bull (over 800 years old!); parish records; historic photographs and plans; glass recipe and pattern books, wonderful maps and even a walking stick. Visitors can discover what the inspiring collections can reveal, join in at amazing events, explore one of the illuminating exhibitions or book a fascinating behind the scenes tour. The centre is also home to Dudley Museum at the Archives and the headquarters of the Black Country UNESCO Global Geopark.

🌐 better.org.uk/library/dudley

✉ customerservices@gll.org

BRIERLEY HILL LIBRARY

Dudley Metropolitan Borough Council/ Better (GLL)

122 High Street, Brierley Hill, DY5 3ET

🌐 better.org.uk/library/dudley

✉ customerservices@gll.org

COSELEY LIBRARY

Dudley Metropolitan Borough Council/ Better (GLL)

Castle Street, Bilston, WV14 9DW

🌐 better.org.uk/library/dudley

✉ customerservices@gll.org

CRADLEY LIBRARY

Dudley Metropolitan Borough Council/ Better (GLL)

Colley Lane, Cradley, Halesowen, B63 2TL

🌐 better.org.uk/library/dudley

✉ customerservices@gll.org

DUDLEY LIBRARY

Dudley Metropolitan Borough Council/ Better (GLL)

St James' Road, Dudley, DY1 1HR

🌐 better.org.uk/library/dudley

✉ customerservices@gll.org

GORNAL LIBRARY

Dudley Metropolitan Borough Council/ Better (GLL)

Abbey Road, Lower Gornal, DY3 2PG

🌐 better.org.uk/library/dudley

✉ customerservices@gll.org

HALESOWEN LIBRARY

Dudley Metropolitan Borough Council/ Better (GLL)

Queensway, Halesowen, B63 4AZ

🌐 better.org.uk/library/dudley

✉ customerservices@gll.org

KINGSWINFORD LIBRARY
Dudley Metropolitan Borough Council/ Better (GLL)
Market Street, Kingswinford, DY6 9LG

🌐 better.org.uk/library/dudley
✉ customerservices@gll.org

LONG LANE LIBRARY
Dudley Metropolitan Borough Council/ Better (GLL)
Long Lane, Halesowen, B62 9JY

🌐 better.org.uk/library/dudley
✉ customerservices@gll.org

LYE LIBRARY
Dudley Metropolitan Borough Council/ Better (GLL)
Chapel Street, Lye, Stourbridge, DY9 8BT

🌐 better.org.uk/library/dudley
✉ customerservices@gll.org

NETHERTON LIBRARY
Dudley Metropolitan Borough Council/ Better (GLL)
The Savoy Centre, Northfield Road, Netherton, DY2 9ES

🌐 better.org.uk/library/dudley
✉ customerservices@gll.org

SEDGLEY LIBRARY
Dudley Metropolitan Borough Council/ Better (GLL)
Ladies Walk, Sedgley, DY3 3UA

🌐 better.org.uk/library/dudley
✉ customerservices@gll.org

STOURBRIDGE LIBRARY
Dudley Metropolitan Borough Council/ Better (GLL)
Crown Centre, Stourbridge, DY8 1YE

🌐 better.org.uk/library/dudley
✉ customerservices@gll.org

WORDSLEY LIBRARY
Dudley Metropolitan Borough Council/ Better (GLL)
Wordsley Green, Stourbridge, DY8 5PD

🌐 better.org.uk/library/dudley
✉ customerservices@gll.org

SANDWELL

Oak House / ©Sandwell Museums

BISHOP ASBURY COTTAGE

Sandwell Metropolitan Borough Council
Newton Road, Great Barr, B43 6HN

The tiny 18th-century workers' cottage was the childhood home of Francis Asbury – one of the most famous people you have probably never heard of! Asbury joined the emerging Methodist movement and after preaching around England went to America. He travelled over a quarter of a million miles spreading the word and was the first Methodist Bishop in the USA. Asbury met George Washington and is considered a founding father of the USA with a statue on the Capitol Hill but is little known in his native land. Visitors to the museum can discover Asbury's fascinating history in prebooked group visits or on heritage open days.

🌐 sandwell.gov.uk/bishopasburycottage
✉ museumarts_tourism@sandwell.gov.uk

Bishop Asbury Cottage / © Sandwell Museums

Bromwich Hall – The Manor House Museum / © Sandwell Museums

BROMWICH HALL – THE MANOR HOUSE MUSEUM

Sandwell Metropolitan Borough Council
Hall Green Road, West Bromwich, B71 2EA

Bromwich Hall was the home of the Lord of the Manor of West Bromwich. The earliest parts of the building date back to the 1270s and the construction of the great hall is believed to be the earliest base cruck in a standing building in the country. There have been some notable residents with fascinating stories including the attorney general to Charles I. There is a lively programme of community events, family activities, community groups, school holiday fun, tours, open days and more throughout the year.

🌐 sandwell.gov.uk/museums

✉ museumarts_tourism@sandwell.gov.uk

GALTON VALLEY PUMPING STATION

Sandwell Metropolitan Borough Council
Brasshouse Lane, Smethwick, B66 1DS

Situated on the Birmingham Main Line Canal, Galton Valley Pumping Station first opened in

Galton Valley Pumping Station / © Sandwell Museums

1892 with the purpose of pumping water from the lower Birmingham New Main Line to the high Old Main Line Canal. This was to replace the water lost from the higher level when boats went through the Smethwick locks. Today this small museum gives an insight into some of the most important and historic civil engineering feats in the area, including the world-famous Galton Bridge, as well as a look at life and work on the canals. The museum is open for monthly open days with regular guided walks to the site of the old Boulton and Watt Engine House.

🌐 sandwell.gov.uk/museums

✉ museumarts_tourism@sandwell.gov.uk

Haden Hill House / ©Sandwell Msueums

HADEN HILL HOUSE MUSEUM AND HADEN OLD HALL

Sandwell Metropolitan Borough Council
Halesowen Road, Cradley Heath, B64 7JU

Haden Hill House Museum in Cradley Heath is a late Victorian gentleman's residence surrounded by 55 acres of parkland. Built by George Alfred Haden Haden-Best in 1878, it was a state of the art residence fit for a 'gentleman' of the period, unlike the Old Hall next door in which George Alfred had grown up. Haden Hill House boasts some fine original features such as the tiled floor in the hallway and Victorian overmantels and is furnished as a Victorian home. There is a lively programme of community events, family fun days, theatre,

live music and school holiday fun throughout the year.

🌐 sandwell.gov.uk/hadenhillhouse
✉ museumarts_tourism@sandwell.gov.uk

OAK HOUSE

Sandwell Metropolitan Borough Council
Oak Road, West Bromwich, B70 8HJ

Oak House in West Bromwich was built in the 1620s by the up and coming Turton family who were nail makers and farmers. A fashionable brick extension was added to the rear in the 1650s as the family wealth and status grew. The house is now furnished and displayed as

Oak House / ©Sandwell Museums

the Turtons may have known it in the later 1600s telling their fascinating story with further information about life in the house in the 1600s. There is a lively programme of community events, family fun days, school holiday activities, live music and much more throughout the year. The house is set in its own grounds which tells more of the site's story with a picnic and play area available to visitors and a tearoom on event and activity days.

🌐 sandwell.gov.uk/oakhouse

✉ museumarts_tourism@sandwell.gov.uk

SANDWELL PRIORY

Sandwell Metropolitan Borough Council
Salters Lane, West Bromwich, B71 4BG

Sandwell Priory was a small medieval Benedictine monastery, founded in the late-12th century by a local landowner. Its remains are now a Scheduled Ancient Monument. Very little remains of the

priory, although its groundplan has been marked out and the layout of the church is fairly clear. There are some low level walls of the structure and the remains of a stone grave that resides in the eastern transept.

🌐 sandwell.gov.uk/info/200248/parks_and_
green_spaces/750/priory_woods

WEDNESBURY MUSEUM AND ART GALLERY

Sandwell Metropolitan Borough Council
Holyhead Road, Wednesbury, WS10 7DF

Wednesbury Museum is Sandwell's Museum and Art Gallery. This purpose built Victorian museum, houses collections ranging from fine art paintings, to one of the world's largest collections of Ruskin pottery. Visitor can also enjoy the Nostalgia Rooms which showcase everyday objects from the 60s and 70s. There is also a changing programme of temporary exhibitions and activities as well as a lively programme of events for all ages, school holiday activities and groups such as community art groups.

🌐 sandwell.gov.uk/museums

✉ museumarts_tourism@sandwell.gov.uk

Guru Nanak Gurdwara Smethwick / ©Guru Nanak Gurdwara Smethwick

FORGE MILL FARM

Sandwell Metropolitan Borough Council
Forge Lane, West Bromwich, B71 3SZ

Set within Sandwell Valley Country Park, Forge Mill Farm is home to a variety of rare breed farm animals. Visitors can explore the farm trail, learn about and feed the animals and enjoy the outdoor children's play area. Other facilities include a farm shop, selling local produce and a maize maze during the summer months.

⊕ sandwell.gov.uk/parks

✉ museumarts_tourism@sandwell.gov.uk

GURU NANAK GURDWARA SMETHWICK

128-130 High St, Smethwick, B66 3AP

Guru Nanak Gurdwara Smethwick is a Sikh place of worship (Gurdwara). Established in 1961 as Europe's first and biggest Gurdwara it remains one of the most prominent and influential Sikh Gurdwaras in the world. Outside sits the Lions of the Great War memorial, unveiled to commemorate 100 years since the end of the First World War. This 10ft high bronze statue is the UK's first to acknowledge the contribution of soldiers from the Indian subcontinent of all faiths, who fought for Britain in both world wars.

⊕ gngsmethwick.com

✉ info@gngsmethwick.com

SANDWELL PARK FARM

Sandwell Metropolitan Borough Council
Salters Lane, West Bromwich, B71 4BG

Sandwell Park Farm is a restored Victorian farm with a historic farmyard and a walled kitchen garden, tearooms and gift shop. It is home to rare and endangered breeds such as Hereford cattle and Bagot goats.

⊕ sandwell.gov.uk/parks

✉ museumarts_tourism@sandwell.gov.uk

Sandwell Park Farm / ©Sandwell MBC

ODEON WEST BROMWICH

New Square, New Street, West Bromwich, B70 7NN

Situated in the heart of West Bromwich, this cinema features five screens showing the latest film releases for all ages. Visitors can also experience the magic of cinema in RealD 3D.

🌐 odeon.co.uk

OLDBURY REP

Barlow Theatre Centre, Spring Walk, Oldbury, B69 4SP

Oldbury Rep in Sandwell is an established community theatre supporting local charities and organisations and also provides a venue for local school productions.

🌐 oldburyrep.org
✉ info@oldburyrep.org

Oldbury Rep / ©Oldbury Rep

BARNFORD PARK

Sandwell Metropolitan Borough Council
Moat Road, Oldbury, B68 8ED

Green Flag Award winning Barnford Park lies a stone's throw from Oldbury town centre. With beautiful parkland offering gentle walks, a children's play area, multi-use games area and community pavilion, there is something on offer for all ages to see and do.

🌐 sandwell.gov.uk/parks

Brunswick Park / ©Birmingham Museums Trust

BRUNSWICK PARK

Sandwell Metropolitan Borough Council
Brunswick Park Road, Wednesbury, WS10 9QR

Brunswick Park was opened in 1887 to celebrate Queen Victoria's golden jubilee. This Green Flag Award winning park offers a range of facilities including outdoor gym equipment, children's play area, multi-games area, tennis courts, skate park, bandstand, football pitches, a pavilion and circular walking trails.

🌐 sandwell.gov.uk/parks

DARTMOUTH PARK

Sandwell Metropolitan Borough Council
Reform Street, West Bromwich, B71 4AS

Dartmouth Park is located between the town centre and Sandwell Valley Country Park. There are plenty of activities for all visitors at this Grade II Listed, Green Flag Award winning park including a fantastic play area, lakes for fishing, and outstanding views across Sandwell Valley, floral displays, a sensory garden, splashpad and a pavilion.

🌐 sandwell.gov.uk/parks

Dartmouth Park / ©Birmingham Museums Trust

Haden Hill Park / ©Birmingham Museums Trust

HADEN HILL PARK

Sandwell Metropolitan Borough Council
Halesowen Road, Cradley Heath, B64 7JU

Green Flag Award winning Haden Hill Park offers a range of things to see and do including playgrounds, pools, a bowling green, great little walks, plenty of wildlife and green spaces plus access to a nature reserve, a Victorian mansion and a Tudor style hall all situated next door to a leisure centre.

🌐 sandwell.gov.uk/parks

LIGHTWOODS PARK

Sandwell Metropolitan Borough Council
Adkins Lane, Bearwood, Smethwick, B67 5DP

This scenic park offers the perfect day out for all ages, with beautiful Shakespeare Gardens, a Grade II Listed bandstand and Grade II Listed house among its attractions. A skate park, and children's play area add to what's on offer in this Green Flag Award winning park.

🌐 sandwell.gov.uk/parks

Lightwoods Park / ©Birmingham Museums Trust

REDHOUSE PARK

Sandwell Metropolitan Borough Council
Hill Lane, Great Barr, B43 6NA

A Green Flag Award winning local area park with facilities including a children's play area, and sports pitches with pavilion and changing rooms.

🌐 sandwell.gov.uk/parks

RSPB SANDWELL VALLEY NATURE RESERVE

RSPB
Tanhouse Avenue, Great Barr, B43 5AG

RSPB Sandwell Valley is a fantastic place to get close to nature. It's perfect for families to have fun together outdoors. Start your adventure at the visitor centre to find out about the latest activities and events, plot your route and get an idea of what wildlife to look out for at this beautiful countryside oasis. There's a lot of nature to explore at RSPB Sandwell Valley. Visitors can enjoy walks along the fully accessible paths, wildlife challenges, activities and natural play features. Wildlife watchers can enjoy exploring the mosaic of habitats, spotting the wildlife that lives here. RSPB Sandwell Valley is also home to a variety of wildlife. Visit the Lakeside Lookout hide to spot wetland birds with the help of friendly guides, hire a kit to go bug hunting or pond dipping (seasonal) or just stroll around taking in seasonal highlights such as dragonflies, fungi, wildflowers and more.

🌐 rspb.org.uk/reserves-and-events/reserves-a-z/sandwell-valley

✉ sandwellvalley@rspb.org.uk

RSPB Sandwell Valley / ©RSPB

Sandwell Valley Country Park / ©Sandwell MBC

SANDWELL VALLEY COUNTRY PARK

Sandwell Metropolitan Borough Council
Salters Lane, West Bromwich, B71 4BG

Situated just a mile from West Bromwich town centre, Sandwell Valley Country Park boasts activities for all. As well as two working farm visitor centres, there are nature areas, an adventure playground, a mountain bike trail, the RSPB visitor centre, woodland, meadows, numerous pools for fishing and farmland. Leisure facilities include an adventure centre with cycle hire, access routes for walking, cycling and horse riding, pitch and putt, crazy golf, tennis courts and football pitches. The Country Park hosts a programme of events including conservation, volunteering, weekly health walks, a summer school holidays fun fair and large-scale shows.

🌐 sandwell.gov.uk/parks

✉ museumarts_tourism@sandwell.gov.uk

SOTS HOLE NATURE RESERVE

Sandwell Metropolitan Borough Council
Temple Meadows Road,
West Bromwich, B71 4DE

Sots Hole is a small fragment of 'semi-ancient' woodland that covers an area of about 13.5 acres. You may well have passed it without realizing it was there. In 1996 it was officially designated a Local Nature Reserve. Sots Hole is for both people and wildlife, offering opportunities to study or learn about nature, or simply just to enjoy it.

🌐 sandwell.gov.uk/parks

VICTORIA PARK, SMETHWICK

Sandwell Metropolitan Borough Council
High Street, Smethwick, B66 3NT

Victoria Park has something that will appeal to all age groups, including children's play areas, cycle routes, cricket square and bandstand. You'll find all the ingredients here for a super day at this Green Flag Award winning park.

🌐 sandwell.gov.uk/parks

WARLEY WOODS

Sandwell Metropolitan Borough Council
The Pavilion, 101 Lightwoods Hill,
Smethwick, B67 5ED

Smethwick's 100-acre Green Flag Award winning park, with its mix of open meadow and nine-hole golf course, has some of the region's most beautiful woodland, offering nature walks, trails, cafe and children's play area.

🌐 sandwell.gov.uk/parks

VICTORIA PARK, TIPTON

Sandwell Metropolitan Borough Council
Victoria Road, Tipton, DY4 8SW

Green Flag Award winning Victoria Park has something for everyone - children's play areas, tennis courts, cricket square, walking routes and wildflower area to name just a few of its attractions.

🌐 sandwell.gov.uk/parks

Warley Woods / ©Birmingham Museums Trust

Victoria Park, Tipton / ©Birmingham Museums Trust

BLACKHEATH LIBRARY

Sandwell Metropolitan Borough Council
145 High Street, Blackheath, Rowley Regis, B65 0EA
🌐 sandwell.gov.uk/libraries
✉ blackheath_library@sandwell.gov.uk

BLEAKHOUSE LIBRARY

Sandwell Metropolitan Borough Council
Bleakhouse Road, Oldbury, B68 9DS
🌐 sandwell.gov.uk/libraries
✉ bleakhouse_library@sandwell.gov.uk

BRANDHALL LIBRARY

Sandwell Metropolitan Borough Council
Tame Road, Oldbury, B68 0JT
🌐 sandwell.gov.uk/libraries
✉ brandhall_library@sandwell.gov.uk

CENTRAL LIBRARY
(WEST BROMWICH)

Sandwell Metropolitan Borough Council
High Street, West Bromwich, B70 8DZ
🌐 sandwell.gov.uk/libraries
✉ central_library@sandwell.gov.uk

CRADLEY HEATH LIBRARY

Sandwell Metropolitan Borough Council
Upper High Street, Cradley Heath, B64 5JU
🌐 sandwell.gov.uk/libraries
✉ cradleyheath_library@sandwell.gov.uk

GLEBEFIELDS LIBRARY

Sandwell Metropolitan Borough Council
St Marks Road, Tipton, DY4 0SZ
🌐 sandwell.gov.uk/libraries
✉ glebefields_library@sandwell.gov.uk

GREAT BARR LIBRARY

Sandwell Metropolitan Borough Council
Birmingham Road, Great Barr, B43 6NW
🌐 sandwell.gov.uk/libraries
✉ greatbarr_library@sandwell.gov.uk

GREAT BRIDGE LIBRARY

Sandwell Metropolitan Borough Council
Sheepwash Lane, Great Bridge, Tipton, DY4 7JF
🌐 sandwell.gov.uk/libraries
✉ greatbridge_library@sandwell.gov.uk

HAMSTEAD LIBRARY

Sandwell Metropolitan Borough Council
Tanhouse Centre, Hamstead Road,
Great Barr, B43 5EL
🌐 sandwell.gov.uk/libraries
✉ hamstead_library@sandwell.gov.uk

HILL TOP LIBRARY

Sandwell Metropolitan Borough Council
Park Buildings, Hill Top, West Bromwich, B70 0RZ
🌐 sandwell.gov.uk/libraries
✉ hilltop_library@sandwell.gov.uk

LANGLEY LIBRARY

Sandwell Metropolitan Borough Council
Barrs Street, Oldbury, B68 8QT
🌐 sandwell.gov.uk/libraries
✉ langley_library@sandwell.gov.uk

STONE CROSS LIBRARY

Sandwell Metropolitan Borough Council
Beverley Road, Stone Cross, West Bromwich, B71 2LH
🌐 sandwell.gov.uk/libraries
✉ stonecross_library@sandwell.gov.uk

OAKHAM LIBRARY

Sandwell Metropolitan Borough Council
Poplar Rise, Tividale, Oldbury, B69 1RD
🌐 sandwell.gov.uk/libraries
✉ oakham_library@sandwell.gov.uk

THIMBLEMILL LIBRARY

Sandwell Metropolitan Borough Council
Thimblemill Road, Smethwick, B67 5RJ
🌐 sandwell.gov.uk/libraries
✉ thimblemill_library@sandwell.gov.uk

OLDBURY LIBRARY

Sandwell Metropolitan Borough Council
Jack Judge House, 10 Halesowen Street,
Oldbury, B69 2AJ
🌐 sandwell.gov.uk/libraries
✉ oldbury_library@sandwell.gov.uk

TIPTON LIBRARY

Sandwell Metropolitan Borough Council
Owen House, 17 Unity Walk, Tipton, DY4 8QL
🌐 sandwell.gov.uk/libraries
✉ tipton_library@sandwell.gov.uk

ROUNDS GREEN LIBRARY

Sandwell Metropolitan Borough Council
Martley Road, Oldbury, B69 1DZ
🌐 sandwell.gov.uk/libraries
✉ roundsgreen_library@sandwell.gov.uk

WEDNESBURY LIBRARY

Sandwell Metropolitan Borough Council
Walsall Street, Wednesbury, WS10 9EH
🌐 sandwell.gov.uk/libraries
✉ wednesbury_library@sandwell.gov.uk

SMETHWICK LIBRARY

Sandwell Metropolitan Borough Council
High Street, Smethwick, B66 1AA
🌐 sandwell.gov.uk/libraries
✉ smethwick_library@sandwell.gov.uk

SOLIHULL

Castle Bromwich Historic Gardens / ©Castle Bromwich Hall Gardens

The National Motorcycle Museum / ©National Motorcycle Museum

THE NATIONAL MOTORCYCLE MUSEUM

Coventry Road, Bickenhill, Solihull, B92 0EJ

The National Motorcycle Museum houses the largest collection of British motorcycles in the world with over 1000 machines from 170 different manufactures spanning no less than three centuries! Of all the machines in the collection there are around 850 on display at any one time throughout the museum's five huge display halls. With the earliest pioneer machine on display dating from 1898, through to the latest British superbikes of this century, the museum collection highlights both the development of the motorcycle as well as showcasing the UK's proud manufacturing heritage.

🌐 thenmm.co.uk

✉ shop@thenmm.co.uk

The Bear Grylls Adventure / ©Jansch Greatrix

THE BEAR GRYLLS ADVENTURE

National Exhibition Centre, Marston Green, B40 1NT

Escape the ordinary, experience the awesome and try something new at The Bear Grylls Adventure, located at Birmingham's NEC. No matter which experience you choose, your adventure guides will inspire you, encourage you and support you through each step of your journey so you can push your limits and reach new achievements with each experience.

🌐 beargryllsadventure.com

✉ info@beargryllsadventure.com

Planet Ice / ©Planet Ice

PLANET ICE SOLIHULL

Hobs Moat Road, Solihull, B92 8JN

Planet Ice is Europe's Number 1 for Ice Leisure. In addition to all the ice related sports and leisure programmes run at Planet Ice Solihull such as Skate Excellence and Hockey Excellence courses, the arenas also host various concerts, shows and alternative sporting events.

🌐 planet-ice.co.uk

✉ solihull@planet-ice.co.uk

The Core Theatre / ©Kirstie Ewes

THE CORE THEATRE

Theatre Square, Touchwood, Homer Road, Solihull, B91 3RG

A multi-purpose arts venue in the heart of Solihull town centre, the Core comprises a 336 seat raked theatre fully equipped technically with stage flying system, sound and lighting. A smaller multi-use studio seating up to 130 is equipped for small-scale theatrical presentations, music events and workshops. The Courtyard Gallery and Art Space is an exhibition space as well as an area for creative activities. The busy venue hosts a varied mix of professional and amateur events including music, drama, comedy and dance.

🌐 thecoretheatresolihull.co.uk

✉ thecoretheatre@solihull.gov.uk

RESORTS WORLD ARENA

NEC Group

Perimeter Road, Birmingham, B40 1NT

Resorts World Arena is the Midlands' outstanding entertainment experience for artists and visitors alike. The venue hosts some of the world's best comedians, sports people, singers, dancers, daredevils and everything in between. With over 100 shows per year and welcoming over 700,000 people each year, Resorts World Arena continues to provide world class entertainment and is regularly home to some of the world's biggest acts who give show-stopping performances at the arena.

🌐 resortsworldarena.co.uk

Babbs Mill Park / ©Solihull MBC

BABBS MILL PARK
Solihull Metropolitan Borough Council
Fordbridge Road, Kingshurst, B37 6LN

A Green Flag Award winning park located in Kingshurst, Babbs Mill Park offers a varied and wild landscape, family play area and many other great facilities including sports courts, walking trails, and regular community events.

🌐 solihull.gov.uk/parks
✉ connectcc@solihull.gov.uk

CASTLE BROMWICH HISTORIC GARDENS
Chester Road, Castle Bromwich, Birmingham B36 9BT

Castle Bromwich Historic Gardens is one of the only examples of unchanged 18th-century formal gardens in the UK. There are over ten acres of 17th- and 18th-century Grade II* Listed walled gardens, wild areas, ponds, vegetable patch and holly maze (a mirror image of the one at Hampton Court Palace designed by George London and Henry Wise) as well as flora and fauna all relating to the time period. The gardens are a breath of fresh air in the city – a healthy place both physically and mentally for visitors; and volunteers. Rescued by volunteers over 35 years ago, the derelict gardens have

been painstakingly restored and maintained back to their original 18th-century beauty.

🌐 castlebromwichhallgardens.org.uk
✉ cbhallgardens@gmail.com

DAMSON LANE PARK
Solihull Metropolitan Borough Council
Damson Lane, Solihull, B92 9JS

Ideally located for the community, Damson Lane Park is a great space for families and friends to relax, play and get fit. The recreation ground features a variety of sports pitches and outdoor gym equipment.

🌐 solihull.gov.uk/parks
✉ parksmanagement@solihull.gov.uk

Castle Bromwich Historic Gardens / ©Holly Rackham

Earlswood Lakes / ©Canal & River Trust

DORRIDGE PARK AND DORRIDGE WOOD LOCAL NATURE RESERVE

Solihull Metropolitan Borough Council
Grange Road, Dorridge, B93 8LJ

Located in the heart of the community, this Green Flag Award winning park, brings the countryside into the area. Complete with a play area which includes traditional yet modern swings and climbing frames.

🌐 solihull.gov.uk/parks
✉ parksmanagement@solihull.gov.uk

EARLSWOOD LAKES

Canal & River Trust
Wood Lane, Solihull, B94 5JH

Earlswood Lakes are the perfect spot to explore local waterside wildlife. Soak up the beautiful scenery while stretching your legs along the towpath, keep an eye out for the historic engine house, admire the striking sailing boats, or take a leisurely stroll down to the local craft centre. The three 22-acre reservoirs – Terry's Pool, Windmill Pool and Engine Pool, are ideal for bird watching – look closely and you might even be lucky enough to spot the rare Lesser Spotted Woodpecker.

🌐 canalrivertrust.org.uk/places-to-visit/
  earlswood-lakes
✉ enquiries.westmidlands@canalrivertrust.org.uk

ELMDON PARK

Solihull Metropolitan Borough Council
Tanhouse Farm Road, Elmdon, B92 9EY

Nestled on the edge of Solihull, Elmdon Nature Park is a wonderful Green Flag Award winning park and Local Nature Reserve. It offers visitors relaxation and adventure amongst the wide open spaces, with a fully equipped play and sports area, which includes swings and roundabout, tennis courts and a football pitch.

🌐 solihull.gov.uk/parks
✉ parksmanagement@solihull.gov.uk

HILLFIELD PARK

Solihull Metropolitan Borough Council
Monkspath Hall Road, Shirley, B91 3LU

A Green Flag Award winning park, Hillfield Park is a wonderful large landscaped area for the local community. Along with a children's play area, the park also features a lake, walking trails and sports pitches.

🌐 solihull.gov.uk/parks
✉ parksmanagement@solihull.gov.uk

KNOWLE PARK

Solihull Metropolitan Borough Council
Lodge Road, Knowle, B93 9HT

A Green Flag Award winning park, Knowle Park provides great open spaces and a play area for families to meet and relax. As a Local Nature Reserve, the park is great for getting in touch with wildlife and features ornamental gardens a play area including springs, zip-wire and climbing net, and tennis courts.

🌐 solihull.gov.uk/parks
✉ parksmanagement@solihull.gov.uk

Elmdon Park / ©Solihull MBC

LAVENDER HALL PARK

Solihull Metropolitan Borough Council
Lavender Hall Lane, Balsall Common, CV7 7BN

Lavender Hall Park boasts Green Flag Award winning status; offering a green haven for everyone in and around Balsall Common Village. With a great playground for children to enjoy, the park is a wonderful space, also boasting sports pitches, a skate park and Katherines Wood, a Local Nature Reserve.

🌐 solihull.gov.uk/parks
✉ parksmanagement@solihull.gov.uk

MALVERN AND BRUETON PARK

Solihull Metropolitan Borough Council
New Road, Solihull, B91 3DL

Two parks in one, Malvern and Brueton Parks, are perfectly located in the town centre. With Green Flag Award winning status, the space offers visitors an easily accessible space to relax and play. With a modern playground, this delightful open space has so much going on. The parks also boast ornamental and sensory gardens, the Parkridge Café, and the Brueton Tree Trail, and hosts regular community events.

🌐 solihull.gov.uk/parks
✉ connectcc@solihull.gov.uk

Malvern Park / ©Solihull MBC

MARSTON GREEN PARK

Solihull Metropolitan Borough Council
Brooklands Way, Marston Green, B37 7FT

At the heart of a vibrant community, Marston Green Park is a wonderful place for families to enjoy, and also explore the local wildlife together. Complete with an excellent playground with swings and carousel, the park also offers multi-sports courts and a wildflower meadow.

🌐 solihull.gov.uk/parks

✉ parksmanagement@solihull.gov.uk

MERIDEN PARK

Solihull Metropolitan Borough Council
Moorend Avenue, Chelmsley Wood, B37 5TB

At the heart of Chelmsley Wood, Meriden Park offers local residents a great mixed use Green Flag Award winning park and Local Nature Reserve throughout the year. With a play area which includes the classic swings and roundabouts, there is also a supervised adventure playground, a skate park, and a variety of sports courts and pitches.

🌐 solihull.gov.uk/parks

✉ parksmanagement@solihull.gov.uk

MILLISON'S WOOD LOCAL NATURE RESERVE

Solihull Metropolitan Borough Council
Albert Road, Meriden, CV5 9AS

Millison's Wood Local Nature Reserve is a wonderful area to see an abundance of wildlife and mature woodland. With an active woodland management scheme in place, Millison's Wood is also home to rare butterflies and birds, and is ideal for walking along a signposted trail.

🌐 solihull.gov.uk/parks

✉ parksmanagement@solihull.gov.uk

OLTON JUBILEE PARK

Solihull Metropolitan Borough Council
Lyndon Road, Olton, B92 7RQ

With large open spaces ideal for family adventures, Olton Jubilee Park is a much-loved community rescource. With swings, rockers and balance beams in the play area, the park also features a BMX track and a variety of sports pitches. The park is also host to a variety of community events throughout the year.

🌐 solihull.gov.uk/parks

✉ parksmanagement@solihull.gov.uk

PARKRIDGE NATURE RESERVE

Warwickshire Wildlife Trust
Warwick Road, Solihull, B91 3HW

The Parkridge Nature Reserve is a tranquil oasis for people and wildlife on the edge of Solihull town centre. Although a modest 5.5 acres, the reserve boasts a variety of popular British and migratory birds including nesting blue tits, woodpeckers, long-tailed tits and nuthatches. Remnants of the historic pleasure grounds include giant redwoods, iron wood trees, black walnut, handkerchief trees, maples and some fine mature oaks. There are several trails around the reserve to help you identify the trees, birds

Parkridge Nature Reserve / ©Solihull MBC

and other exciting features. There is also a fun adventure playground for children of all ages to enjoy, a mud kitchen and a variety of children's activities.

🌐 warwickshirewildlifetrust.org.uk/Parkridge

✉ enquiries@wkwt.org.uk

SHIRLEY PARK

Solihull Metropolitan Borough Council
Stratford Road, Shirley, B90 3AL

A Green Flag Award winning park lying in the centre of the local region's busy shopping area, Shirley Park offers a space for recreation and a welcome green space in this urban setting. With an outdoor gym, community artwork, ornamental gardens, a variety of sports courts and pitches, along with a dog agility area, there is something for everyone.

The park also boasts a children's play area and a skate park, and hosts events through the summer.

🌐 solihull.gov.uk/parks

✉ connectcc@solihull.gov.uk

TUDOR GRANGE PARK

Solihull Metropolitan Borough Council
Monkspath Hall Road, Solihull, B91 3LU

Ideally located for Solihull town centre, this Green Flag Award winning park is perfect for relaxing and having fun with friends and family. With its cycle track, pitch and putt course, children's play area and skate park there is a great deal to enjoy at Tudor Grange.

🌐 solihull.gov.uk/parks

✉ parksmanagement@solihull.gov.uk

The Core Library / ©Solihull MBC

BALSALL COMMON LIBRARY

Solihull Metropolitan Borough Council
283 Kenilworth Road, Balsall Common, CV7 7EL

🌐 solihull.gov.uk/libraries
✉ libraryarts@solihull.gov.uk

CASTLE BROMWICH LIBRARY

Solihull Metropolitan Borough Council
Hurst Lane North, Castle Bromwich, B36 0EY

🌐 solihull.gov.uk/libraries
✉ libraryarts@solihull.gov.uk

CHELMSLEY WOOD LIBRARY

Solihull Metropolitan Borough Council
10 West Mall, Chelmsley Wood Shopping Centre,
Chelmsley Wood, B37 5TN

🌐 solihull.gov.uk/libraries
✉ libraryarts@solihull.gov.uk

THE CORE LIBRARY

Solihull Metropolitan Borough Council
Homer Road, Solihull, B91 3RG

The Core Library is the main library for Solihull, providing a wide range of books for adults, young adults and children, a large Heritage and Local Studies collection for Solihull, reference and information sources, and free computer access for library members. Regular childrens' events are held including Storytime and Rhymetimes. The Core also houses the Core Theatre, the Encore cafe-bar, the Community Advice Hub and the Solihull Connect one-stop-shop for council services.

🌐 solihull.gov.uk/libraries
✉ libraryarts@solihull.gov.uk

DICKENS HEATH LIBRARY
Solihull Metropolitan Borough Council
Old Dickens Heath Road, Dickens Heath, B90 1SD
🌐 solihull.gov.uk/libraries
✉ libraryarts@solihull.gov.uk

MARSTON GREEN LIBRARY
Solihull Metropolitan Borough Council
Land Lane, Birmingham, B37 7DQ
🌐 solihull.gov.uk/libraries
✉ libraryarts@solihull.gov.uk

HAMPTON IN ARDEN LIBRARY
Solihull Metropolitan Borough Council
39 Fentham Road, Hampton in Arden, B92 0AY
🌐 solihull.gov.uk/libraries
✉ libraryarts@solihull.gov.uk

MERIDEN LIBRARY
Solihull Metropolitan Borough Council
Arden Cottage, The Green, Meriden, CV7 7LN
🌐 solihull.gov.uk/libraries
✉ libraryarts@solihull.gov.uk

HOBS MOAT LIBRARY
Solihull Metropolitan Borough Council
Ulleries Road, Solihull, B92 8EB
🌐 solihull.gov.uk/libraries
✉ libraryarts@solihull.gov.uk

OLTON LIBRARY
Solihull Metropolitan Borough Council
169A Warwick Road, Olton, B92 7AR
🌐 solihull.gov.uk/libraries
✉ libraryarts@solihull.gov.uk

KINGSHURST LIBRARY
Solihull Metropolitan Borough Council
Marston Drive, Kingshurst, B37 6BD
🌐 solihull.gov.uk/libraries
✉ libraryarts@solihull.gov.uk

SHIRLEY LIBRARY
Solihull Metropolitan Borough Council
22 Parkgate, Stratford Road, Shirley, B90 3GG
🌐 solihull.gov.uk/libraries
✉ libraryarts@solihull.gov.uk

KNOWLE LIBRARY
Solihull Metropolitan Borough Council
Chester House, 1667-1669 High Street,
Knowle, B93 0LL
🌐 solihull.gov.uk/libraries
✉ libraryarts@solihull.gov.uk

WALSALL

Chasewater Railway / *©Alistair Grieve/Chasewater Railway*

Aldridge Transport Museum / ©Aldridge Transport Museum

ALDRIDGE TRANSPORT MUSEUM

Shenstone Drive, Aldridge, WS9 8TP

Explore the history of transport through a wide range of vehicles including buses, commercial vehicles, private cars as well as transport memorabilia – all with a West Midlands connection. Visitors will see vehicles in various stages of restoration, and even have the opportunity to take a trip one of the museums restored buses.

🌐 amrtm.org

✉ amrtm1@aol.co.uk

THE NEW ART GALLERY WALSALL

Walsall Council
Gallery Square, Walsall, WS2 8LG

The New Art Gallery Walsall presents, collects and interprets historic, modern and contemporary art in innovative and challenging ways, welcoming visitors from all over the globe as well as the immediate locality. The changing exhibition programmes on Floors 3 and 4 focus on the contemporary visual arts. Presenting

The New Art Gallery Walsall / ©The New Art Gallery Walsall

both solo and group shows and reflecting the diversity of current practice, the programme seeks to support the development of living artists and to engage and challenge visitors. The galleries were specifically designed to house The Garman Ryan collection, gifted to the people of Walsall by Lady Kathleen Garman, widow of Sir Jacob Epstein, and her friend, Sally Ryan. With a strong family focus, the Collection includes both European and non-European works and includes paintings, drawings, sculpture and prints by artists such as Picasso, Braque, Gericault and Delacroix.

🌐 thenewartgallerywalsall.org.uk

✉ info@thenewartgallerywalsall.org.uk

WALSALL LEATHER MUSEUM
Walsall Council
Littleton Street West, Walsall, WS2 8EW

Discover why Walsall became the British leather goods capital in this fascinating working museum, housed in a restored leather factory. The people of Walsall have been making some of the world's finest saddles and leather goods for over two hundred years. Walsall Leather Museum celebrates the great achievements of local leather craftsmen and women, and tells the story of the Walsall leather trade. Displays feature examples of historic craftsmanship and exciting contemporary designs.

🌐 go.walsall.gov.uk/leathermuseum
✉ leathermuseum@walsall.gov.uk

Walsall Leather Museum / ©Walsall Council

Chasewater Railway / ©Alistair Grieve/Chasewater Railway

CHASEWATER RAILWAY
Brownhills West Station, Pool Lane, Walsall, WS8 7NL

With almost four miles of track circumnavigating Chasewater, take a trip into neighbouring Staffordshire on this vintage railway operating standard gauge heritage steam and diesel trains. Part of the route lies on the trackbed of the former Midland Railway's branch from Aldridge through Brownhills that serviced the collieries that once operated in the area. Trains run on weekends and Bank Holidays throughout the year (check the website for latest service information, and for special events). The headquarters is host to a museum and heritage centre, a model railway, The Sidings Tearooms (open Wednesday - Sunday) and a gift shop.

🌐 chasewaterrailway.co.uk
✉ admin@chasewaterrailway.co.uk

Chasewater Railway / ©Alistair Grieve/Chasewater Railway

WALSALL ARENA AND ARTS CENTRE

Hawbush Road, Leamore, Walsall, WS3 1AG

Walsall Arena and Arts Centre (formerly known as the Forest Arts Centre), is Walsall's number one activity hub for participatory and performing arts. Whether you want to learn, perform or just sit back and enjoy the show Walsall Arena and Arts Centre is the place to come. The Arts Centre has state-of-the-art facilities including two auditoriums, dance studio, community cinema, recording studio, digital arts suite, sound proofed rehearsal rooms, arts classrooms and conference suites.

🌐 walsallarena.com

Walsall Arena and Arts Centre / ©Walsall Council

Barr Beacon / ©Walsall Council

BARR BEACON LOCAL NATURE RESERVE

Walsall Council

Beacon Road, Aldridge Walsall, WS9 0QW

Only three miles from Walsall town centre, Barr Beacon is one of the highest points in the West Midlands. It offers spectacular panoramic views, and from the top you can see surrounding landmarks including the Wrekin, Cannock Chase, Lichfield Cathedral, Birmingham City Centre, and the Lickey Hills. It is the high-point of the Beacon Way and a favourite walking spot for locals. The reserve also features Beacon War Memorial and a number of nature trails.

🌐 go.walsall.gov.uk/parks_and_green_spaces
✉ healthyspaces@walsall.gov.uk

Barr Beacon View / ©Walsall Council

BROWNHILLS COMMON NATURE RESERVE

Walsall Council

The Parade, Brownhills, WS8 7NG

Brownhills Common is a fine example of lowland heath, which is home to a wealth of wildlife from deer and rabbits, to lizards and even Great Crested Newts. Among its 100 acres visitors can discover a variety of species of birds and find wild flowers growing here that can only be found on heathland.

🌐 go.walsall.gov.uk/parks_and_green_spaces

✉ healthyspaces@walsall.gov.uk

CLAYHANGER COMMON

Walsall Council

28 Ennerdale Close, Clayhanger, WS8 7SB

An abundance of wildlife can be found at Clayhanger Common. This reclaimed beauty spot is home to ducks and moorhens, and flowering waterplants including arrowhead and flowering rush, which thrive in the clean water of the Wyrely & Essington Canal. Part of the common has been designated a Site of

Importance for Nature Conservation and you will find heather, birch and willow flourishing in the acidic grassland together with the damp-loving common spotted orchids and the locally rare ragged robin in the drainage ditches which cross the site. The wet grassland areas have pools which are home to a large population of smooth newts.

🌐 go.walsall.gov.uk/parks_and_green_spaces

✉ healthyspaces@walsall.gov.uk

CUCKOO'S NOOK AND THE DINGLE LOCAL NATURE RESERVE

Walsall Council

Sutton Road, Walsall, WS9 0TA

A walk through Cuckoo's Nook and the Dingle Local Nature Reserve will take you through two completely different habitats, created by two different types of soil, and will transport you across 60 million years of geological time. The reserve lies over a geological fault line, where on one side, coal measures lie near the surface, and on the other, limestone, having a direct effect on the plant life that you'll find above the

Brownhills Common / ©Walsall Council

soil. Cuckoo's Nook is an ancient semi-natural acidic woodland, with species like holly, oak, birch and alder and is also a bluebell woodland flushed with bluish-purple in May each year! Walk along into the Dingle, however, and you'll find yourself surrounded by hawthorn, ash, beech, elder and large-leaved lime trees, which love the alkaline limestone soil. Cuckoo's Nook and the Dingle is a great place to learn about geology – you might even find fossils there, as there are exposed Silurian limestone beds in the Dingle!

🌐 go.walsall.gov.uk/parks_and_green_spaces

✉ healthyspaces@walsall.gov.uk

Cuckoos' Nook/ ©Walsall Council

FIBBERSLEY LOCAL NATURE RESERVE

Walsall Council

Noose Lane, Willenhall, WV13 3BJ

Fibbersley is one of Walsall's finest wetland sites. Visitors to this Green Flag Award winning green space can find a network of pools of various sizes, which are home to a variety of aquatic life, from insects like diving beetles and dragonflies, to amphibians.

🌐 go.walsall.gov.uk/parks_and_green_spaces

✉ healthyspaces@walsall.gov.uk

Fibbersley Nature Reserve/ ©Walsall Council

GEORGE ROSE PARK

Walsall Council

188 Wolverhampton Street, Darlaston, WS10 8UB

George Rose Park is a large green with formal park area and a historic park lodge, bandstand, play area, and trim trail for outdoor exercise. It has a strip of flatter grassland used for sporting activities, as well as being hired out regularly for events over the summer months.

🌐 go.walsall.gov.uk/parks_and_green_spaces

✉ healthyspaces@walsall.gov.uk

HAY HEAD WOOD LOCAL NATURE RESERVE
Walsall Council
Longwood Lane, Walsall, WS4 2JS

This 17-acre site contains an interesting mixture of woodland, wetland and grassland habitats. The site has been declared a Local Nature Reserve, giving it greater protection for the future.

🌐 go.walsall.gov.uk/parks_and_green_spaces
✉ healthyspaces@walsall.gov.uk

Hay Head Wood / ©Walsall Council

KINGS HILL PARK
Walsall Council
Forge Road, Wednesbury, WS10 7TP

Kings Hill Park in Darlaston is one of Walsall's area green spaces. This Green Flag Award winning park has a children's play area, picnic area, and a mix of wooded and open areas of grassland to the south of the park. There are also junior football pitches and changing rooms available for hire. The park is host to various different community events and activities throughout the year.

🌐 go.walsall.gov.uk/parks_and_green_spaces
✉ healthyspaces@walsall.gov.uk

Leigh's Wood/ ©Walsall Council

LEIGH'S WOOD NATURE RESERVE
Walsall Council
Northgate, Aldridge, WS9 8XU

Leigh's Wood in Aldridge is one of Walsall smallest countryside sites, at around 12 acres. It is a woodland of mainly birch and oak trees, and it is home to a wide variety of birds, plants and insects. It is also one of Walsall's bluebell woodlands (along with Merrions Wood and Cuckoos Nook), so it is a fantastic place to go to look for signs of Spring. The wood also has a pond where you'll find even more wildlife, such as ducks and moorhens. The woodland is home to many species of bird, and mammals including hedgehogs. The site also features nature trails, a children's play area and skate park.

🌐 go.walsall.gov.uk/parks_and_green_spaces
✉ healthyspaces@walsall.gov.uk

MERRIONS WOOD LOCAL NATURE RESERVE
Walsall Council
Skip Lane, Walsall, B43 7AN

Merrions Wood Local Nature Reserve is a 30-acre Green Flag Award winning open space located just to the south east of Walsall town centre. It is predominantly a mature oak and beech woodland, with some fields and associated hedgerows. Bordered by housing immediately to the south, the open countryside extends south westwards towards Sandwell Valley, and northwards to Barr Beacon and beyond. The site forms part of the Great Barr Conservation Area, and is designated a Site of Importance to Nature Conservation.

🌐 go.walsall.gov.uk/parks_and_green_spaces
✉ healthyspaces@walsall.gov.uk

MOORCROFT WOOD LOCAL NATURE RESERVE
Walsall Council
Hawkswood Drive, Darlaston, WS10 8GA

One of only a few countryside sites on the west side of the Borough, Moorcroft Wood Local Nature Reserve is a secret haven full of insects and other wildlife, and an amazing landscape reminding us of its geology and incredible industrial past.

🌐 go.walsall.gov.uk/parks_and_green_spaces
✉ healthyspaces@walsall.gov.uk

Merrions Wood / ©Birmingham Museums Trust

Palfrey Park / ©Walsall Council

PALFREY PARK

Walsall Council
69 Dale Street, Palfrey, WS1 4AN

As one of Walsall's flagship green spaces, Palfrey Park is a significant local landmark. This Green Flag Award winning park boasts a wide range of facilities and features including a children's play area with picnic and seating area, bowling green, two grass volleyball courts, sports pitches and a nature conservation area incorporating a pond, dipping platform, woodland, wildflower meadow and walking trails.

🌐 go.walsall.gov.uk/parks_and_green_spaces
✉ healthyspaces@walsall.gov.uk

Park Lime Pits / ©Walsall Council

PARK LIME PITS LOCAL NATURE RESERVE

Walsall Council
Park Road, Walsall, WS4 2HH

Park Lime Pits Local Nature Reserve is the perfect peaceful urban getaway. A walk around its tranquil pools and mature woodland belies its busy past as a quarry, when the limestone within was used to support the industrial revolution, and a busy network of canals connected the pits to iron foundries around the Black Country. These days, rather than the sounds of industry, you're likely to hear the sound of great spotted woodpeckers hammering away in the trees, and the occasional splash of a fish in the big pool. It's still adjacent to the canal, and as such it's a frequent stopping point for people walking or cycling the canal towpaths between the Arboretum and Chasewater.

🌐 go.walsall.gov.uk/parks_and_green_spaces
✉ healthyspaces@walsall.gov.uk

PELSALL NORTH COMMON LOCAL NATURE RESERVE

Walsall Council
Pelsall North Common, Pelsall, WS3 5AA

Pelsall North Common Local Nature Reserve is one of the most valuable wildlife sites in the borough. Like its neighbour, Brownhills Common, it is an area of wet lowland heath, an increasingly rare habitat that supports a vast array of wildlife

from specialist heathland butterflies and bees to a wide variety of birds and mammals.

🌐 go.walsall.gov.uk/parks_and_green_spaces
✉ healthyspaces@walsall.gov.uk

PELSALL VILLAGE COMMON

Walsall Council
Vicarage Road, Pelsall, WS3 4AZ

Pelsall Village Common is a large and well used public open space, nestled just south of Pelsall High Street. The site is unique in that it is split into four. The north west quarter, features a children's play area; and the north east quarter of the site is used extensively by sporting teams, and is also flat enough to cater for carnival and funfair events in the summer.

🌐 go.walsall.gov.uk/parks_and_green_spaces
✉ healthyspaces@walsall.gov.uk

Pelsall North Common / ©Walsall Council

Pelsall Village Common / ©Walsall Council

PLECK PARK
Walsall Council
Montfort Road, Walsall, WS2 9DE

Pleck Park is a large and well used public open space. The site has a wide range of facilities including a children's play area, tennis courts, basketball courts, BMX track, and a multipurpose games area; as well as a large field space which supports cricket and football events.

🌐 go.walsall.gov.uk/parks_and_green_spaces

✉ healthyspaces@walsall.gov.uk

REEDSWOOD PARK
Walsall Council
Reedswood Gardens, Walsall, WS2 8SP

Reedswood Park is a large park close to the Crown Wharf end of Walsall town centre and the Reedswood Retail Park. As well as a formal park area with a children's play area, football and cricket pitches, and a circular path making for a perfect health walk, the site is bordered by woodland, which to the north leads to Reedswood Fishing Pool and the Victory Pools Site of Importance to Nature Conservation.

🌐 go.walsall.gov.uk/parks_and_green_spaces

✉ healthyspaces@walsall.gov.uk

ROUGH WOOD CHASE
Walsall Council
41 Pooles Lane, Willenhall, WV12 5HJ

Green Flag Award winning Rough Wood Chase is made up of six separate nature reserves, which lie on the western edge of Walsall Borough. It comprises Rough Wood (the largest oak woodland in Walsall), Bentley Haye, Wood Farm, the Piggeries, Sneyd Reservoir and Oily Goughs. Rough Wood Chase also includes Beechdale Park, despite it not being a formally designated Local Nature Reserve, and the site is also adjacent to a popular fishing site, Bailey's Pool.

🌐 go.walsall.gov.uk/parks_and_green_spaces

✉ healthyspaces@walsall.gov.uk

Pleck Park / ©Walsall Council

STUBBERS GREEN
Walsall Council
Stubbers Green Road, Shelfield, WS9 8BQ

Stubbers Green is one of Walsall's post-industrial countryside sites, comprising of pools (Swan Pool and the Swag) that used to be quarry pits. Today the area has become a haven for all kinds of bird life, from ducks, geese and swans to reed-nesting birds like Reed Warblers. Stubbers Green boasts an impressive species list of waders, ducks and other birds, to the extent that it has been recognised for its importance as a habitat for reed-nesting birds and as a roosting site for birds like swallows.

🌐 go.walsall.gov.uk/parks_and_green_spaces
✉ healthyspaces@walsall.gov.uk

WALSALL ARBORETUM
Walsall Council
Lichfield Street, Walsall, WS4 2BU

Walsall Arboretum is a Victorian public park located close to the town. Part of the park and surrounding housing are covered by the Arboretum conservation area. The park features a bandstand, boathouse and pedalos, cricket pitch, skatepark, splash pad and cafe.

🌐 go.walsall.gov.uk/parks_and_green_spaces
✉ healthyspaces@walsall.gov.uk

Walsall Arboretum / ©Walsall Council

Stubbers Green / ©Walsall Council

Walsall Arboretum / ©Walsall Council

WILLENHALL MEMORIAL PARK

Walsall Council

31 Pinson Road, Willenhall, WV13 2PW

Created in the 1920s as a tribute to locals who
died in the First World War, this Green Flag
Award winning park features a children's play
area, skate park, outdoor gym, splash pad,
community pavilion and cafe.

🌐 go.walsall.gov.uk/parks_and_green_spaces

✉ healthyspaces@walsall.gov.uk

Willenhall Memorial Park / ©Walsall Council

ALDRIDGE DISTRICT LIBRARY

Walsall Council

Rookery Lane, Aldridge, WS9 8NP

🌐 go.walsall.gov.uk/walsalllibraries/Our-Libraries

✉ aldridgelibrary@walsall.gov.uk

BLOXWICH DISTRICT LIBRARY

Walsall Council

Elmore Row, Bloxwich, WS3 2HR

🌐 go.walsall.gov.uk/walsalllibraries/Our-Libraries

✉ bloxwichlibrary@walsall.gov.uk

BROWNHILLS DISTRICT LIBRARY

Walsall Council

Park View Centre, Chester Road North, Brownhills, WS8 7JB

🌐 go.walsall.gov.uk/walsalllibraries/Our-Libraries

✉ brownhillslibrary@walsall.gov.uk

DARLASTON DISTRICT LIBRARY

Walsall Council

1 King Street, Darlaston, WS10 8DE

🌐 go.walsall.gov.uk/walsalllibraries/Our-Libraries

✉ darlastonlibrary@walsall.gov.uk

LICHFIELD ST HUB

Walsall Council

Lichfield Street Hub (Walsall Central Library & Archives), Lichfield Street, Walsall, WS1 1TR

🌐 go.walsall.gov.uk/walsalllibraries/Our-Libraries

✉ LSHlibrary@walsall.gov.uk

STREETLY COMMUNITY LIBRARY

Walsall Council

Blackwood Road, Streetly, B74 3PL

🌐 go.walsall.gov.uk/walsalllibraries/Our-Libraries

✉ streetlylibrary@walsall.gov.uk

WILLENHALL DISTRICT LIBRARY

Walsall Council

Walsall Street Willenhall, WV13 2EX

🌐 go.walsall.gov.uk/walsalllibraries/Our-Libraries

✉ willenhalllibrary@walsall.gov.uk

WOLVERHAMPTON

Moseley Old Hall / ©National Trust

Bantock House Museum / ©City of Wolverhampton

BANTOCK HOUSE MUSEUM

City of Wolverhampton Council
Finchfield Road, Wolverhampton, WV3 9LQ

Restored to its Edwardian glory, Bantock House is a hidden treasure set within 43 acres of parkland and surrounded by delightful formal gardens. Visit Bantock House Museum and explore the history of Wolverhampton and its people in the period settings of the former Bantock family home. Complete with carved oak panelled rooms, decorative glass, tiles and period furnishings inspired by the Arts and Crafts movement, lives are revealed alongside displays of locally made enamels, japanned ware, jewellery, toys, dolls and Pre-Raphaelite paintings.

🌐 wolverhamptonart.org.uk
✉ bantock.house@wolverhampton.gov.uk

BILSTON GALLERY

City of Wolverhampton Council
Mount Pleasant, Bilston, WV14 7LU

Contemporary craft exhibitions and displays of historic items created by skilled makers, plus events for all age. Bilston Gallery features a fantastic display that showcases everything that makes the Black Country the place it is, from the incredible range of fossils and minerals, to the inspired creativity of cut steel jewellery, and the world famous Bilston enamels.

🌐 wolverhamptonart.org.uk
✉ bilston.craftgallery@wolverhampton.gov.uk

Bilston Craft Gallery / ©City of Wolverhampton

Moseley Old Hall / ©City of Wolverhampton

MOSELEY OLD HALL

National Trust
Moseley Old Hall Lane, Fordhouses, WV10 7HY

Moseley Old Hall is famous as one of the resting places of Charles II during his escape to France during the English Civil War. In this atmospheric Elizabethan farmhouse that saved a king, visitors can explore the dramatic story of the king hiding from Cromwell's troops at Moseley Old Hall after he fled the Battle of Worcester in 1651. See the bed on which the king slept and the priest hole in which he hid, and hear fascinating stories about what life was like in the 17th-century from tour guides and costumed interpreters. A variety of 17th-century plants, a fruit orchard and a striking knot garden adorn the graceful gardens. Further into King's Walk Wood there is a tree-hide for children of all ages to explore.

🌐 nationaltrust.org.uk/moseley-old-hall
✉ moseleyoldhall@nationaltrust.org.uk

Tettenhall Transport Heritage Centre /
©Tettenhall Transport heritage Centre

TETTENHALL TRANSPORT HERITAGE CENTRE

35, Blakeley Avenue, Wolverhampton, WV6 9HR

Home to many intriguing pieces of transport history, the Heritage Centre is the first transport museum in the city of Wolverhampton, run by the community for the community.

🌐 steamheritage.co.uk/museums-and-attractions/entry/tettenhall-transport-heritage-centre

✉ alecbrew@hotmail.co.uk

WIGHTWICK MANOR AND GARDENS

National Trust
Wightwick Bank, Wolverhampton, WV6 8BN

Discover the legacy of a family's passion for Victorian art and design and delve into Wightwick Manor's remarkable history and stunning collection of Pre-Raphaelite paintings by Rossetti, Burne-Jones and their followers. Visitors can take a step back in time and visit this ever-changing family home that's also a beautiful art gallery. You may need to book in advance, please see website for most up to date information.

🌐 nationaltrust.org.uk/wightwick-manor-and-gardens

✉ wightwickmanor@nationaltrust.org.uk

WOLVERHAMPTON ART GALLERY

City of Wolverhampton Council
Lichfield Street, Wolverhampton, WV1 1DU

The city centre art gallery is packed with inspiring and uplifting paintings, and holds the largest collection of Pop Art outside of London.

Wightwick Manor / © National Trust

Wolverhampton Art Gallery / ©City of Wolverhampton

Visitors can explore more than 300 years of art in the free gallery with fantastic changing exhibitions and permanent galleries of both Georgian and Victorian paintings.

🌐 wolverhamptonart.org.uk

✉ art.gallery@wolverhampton.gov.uk

WOLVERHAMPTON CITY ARCHIVES

City of Wolverhampton Council
Whitmore Hill, Wolverhampton, WV1 1SF

Explore the rich life of Wolverhampton and its people through Wolverhampton City Archives. Housing a wealth of materials relating to the history of all areas now within the city of Wolverhampton including Bilston, Bushbury, Penn, Tettenhall and Wednesfield. Constantly growing, the vast collections include maps, books, census returns, newspapers, records from local schools, churches, clubs, societies and businesses, electoral registers, and indexes to births, deaths and marriages. There are also over 30,000 photographs, plus films, sound recordings, memorabilia and much more. A

Wolverhampton City Archives / ©City of Wolverhampton

city landmark, this Grade II* Listed building was built in the mid-18th century as a home for the wealthy Molineux family, before becoming a hotel in the 1870s. Having fallen into disrepair after closing in 1979, the building has since been fully restored, with the impressive wood panelled Oak Room and ornate Rococo Room giving a glimpse into the former life of the building.

🌐 wolverhamptonart.org.uk

✉ archives@wolverhampton.gov.uk

Bratch Locks / ©Canal & River Trust

BRATCH LOCKS
Canal & River Trust
104 Bratch Lane, WV5 8DH

Bratch Locks, originally built as a staircase, are the perfect spot for a family day out, exploring the Staffordshire & Worcestershire Canal's history and local wildlife. Take a walk along the towpath and admire the historic bridge and the Bratch pumping station, or enjoy the abundance of greenery. If you love wildlife, follow the exciting bat trail, or keep an eye out for some of the canals other natural residents like kingfishers or dragonflies. If you look carefully, you might even spot an otter.

🌐 canalrivertrust.org.uk/places-to-visit/the-bratch

✉ enquiries.westmidlands@canalrivertrust.org.uk

WILD ZOOLOGICAL PARK
Upper Whittimere Farm, Tom Lane,
Halfpenny Green, DY7 5EP

WILD Zoological Park was born out of a dream to educate the public about different animals, poke holes in common misconceptions and

Wild Zoological Park / ©Wild Zoological Park

to remove stigmas commonly associated with animals that aren't so cute and fluffy. The animals and staff at WILD Zoological Park are here to conserve wildlife and teach people about all forms of wildlife, with the hope that through teaching and deeper understanding, there will be a stronger drive to help us conserve the world's wildlife. With a variety of live shows and displays, the park is also home to the UK's largest free flight bird show with over 100 birds flying overhead in each display.

🌐 wildzoo.co.uk

✉ info@wildzoo.co.uk

ARENA THEATRE

Wulfruna Street, Wolverhampton, WV1 1SE

The Arena Theatre is situated on the University of Wolverhampton's city campus. The main auditorium seats 150 people and is used for both professional touring shows and for local community groups. The Arena is a small-scale theatre with a great informal atmosphere for all visitors. It presents one of the most diverse theatre programmes in the West Midlands, and top quality professional productions, local and amateur shows alike create and exciting array of performances each year.

🌐 wlv.ac.uk/arena-theatre

✉ arena@wlv.ac.uk

Grand Theatre / ©City of Wolverhampton

Civic Hall / ©City of Wolverhampton

CIVIC HALL & WULFEN HALL

City of Wolverhampton Council
North Street, Wolverhampton, WV1 1RQ

Wolves Civic and sister venue Wulfrun Hall form a major hub for live entertainment in Wolverhampton and the Black Country. The 3,000 capacity Civic Hall was originally opened in 1938 and has hosted a wide variety of acts and events.

🌐 wolvescivic.co.uk

✉ events.enquiries@wolverhampton.gov.uk

GRAND THEATRE

City of Wolverhampton Council
Lichfield Street, Wolverhampton, WV1 1DE

The Wolverhampton Grand Theatre, commonly known as The Grand, is located on Lichfield Street. Designed in 1894 by Architect Charles J. Phipps, it lives up to its name and is a Grade II Listed Building with a seating capacity of 1200.

🌐 grandtheatre.co.uk

✉ feedback@grandtheatre.co.uk

LIGHT HOUSE MEDIA CENTRE

Suite 16, Chubb Building, Fryer Street, WV1 1HT

Light House, the Black Country's only independent cinema, is a charity and arts venue which aims to increase the enjoyment and understanding of technologically-based media, in particular film, video, photography

Newhampton Arts Centre / ©Newhampton Arts Centre

and creative media and to emphasise their importance to the cultural, social and economic life of Wolverhampton, and the West Midlands. A cultural hub, it houses two photography galleries, a live events programme and cinemas of 240 and 67 seats.

🌐 light-house.co.uk/LightHouseMediaCentre. dll/Home

✉ kelly@light-house.co.uk

NEWHAMPTON ARTS CENTRE
Dunkley Street, Wolverhampton, WV14AN

The NAC (Newhampton Arts Centre) is a creative venue in the heart of Wolverhampton that nurtures new talent and new ideas. With a wide range of facilities, it offers opportunities to enjoy and engage in the arts. As a creative hub, it supports 30 resident organisations. The NAC is a registered charity and is accessible and open to everyone.

🌐 newhamptonarts.co.uk

✉ office@newhamptonarts.co.uk

Slade Room / ©City of Wolverhampton

SLADE ROOM
City of Wolverhampton Council
Broad Street, Wolverhampton, WV1 1HP

The Slade Rooms (previously known as The Little Civic) is a 550-capacity venue in the heart of the city which was opened in 2010 by the band who inspired its name.

🌐 www.wolvescivic.co.uk

✉ events.enquiries@wolverhampton.gov.uk

Hickman Park / ©City of Wolverhampton

BANTOCK PARK

City of Wolverhampton Council
Finchfield Road, Wolverhampton, WV3 9LQ

Bantock Park is a great venue for a range of activities at low or no cost. A picnic in the park is something the whole family can enjoy. The children's play area has many challenges for young children, for example, traditional monkey bars and swings to multi-play units. The park also features a nine hole pitch and putt course.

🌐 wolverhampton.gov.uk/visiting/parks-green-spaces-and-nature-reserves

HICKMAN PARK

City of Wolverhampton Council
Wolverhampton Street, Bilston, WV14 0LZ

Hickman park is located half a mile from Bilston town centre. The park boasts a sports arena with terracing, ideal for both playing sports and for spectators. In addition there are walking trails and a children's play area along with sports pitches and a wildflower meadow.

🌐 wolverhampton.gov.uk/visiting/parks-green-spaces-and-nature-reserves

EAST PARK

City of Wolverhampton Council
Hickman Avenue, Wolverhampton, WV1 2BS

East Park is one of Wolverhampton's district parks and has a proud history, going back to 1896. Facilities include football pitches, a children's play area, paddling pool and tennis courts.

🌐 wolverhampton.gov.uk/visiting/parks-green-spaces-and-nature-reserves

NORTHYCOTE FARM

City of Wolverhampton Council
Underhill Lane, Bushbury, WV10 7JF

There are many informal walks through the woodland at Northycote which offer opportunities to view or photograph a wide variety of wildlife in their natural habitats. Animals at the farm include Norfolk Black turkeys, geese, Shropshire sheep and pigs.

🌐 wolverhampton.gov.uk/visiting/parks-green-spaces-and-nature-reserves

Northycote Farm / ©City of Wolverhampton

PENDEFORD MILL NATURE RESERVE

City of Wolverhampton Council
Pendeford Hall Lane, Coven,
Wolverhampton, WV9 5ET

Pendeford Mill Nature Reserve is a site of valuable environmental and historical significance. The site covers 60 acres of naturally managed countryside and dates back to the 13th-century. It provides a stable and protected habitat for wildlife on the fringe of an urban area. Among the woodland is an impressive yew tree which experts have dated back to 2,000 years old. The tree is also home to a rare species of bat. Nearby are towering oak trees – a little younger at around 400-years old. A stunning pool with its own island, the fish-filled River Penk and the chance to spot rare birds, badgers, plants and marvellous mini-beasts make Pendeford Mill Nature Reserve a very special spot indeed.

 wolverhampton.gov.uk/visiting/parks-green-spaces-and-nature-reserves

SMESTOW VALLEY LOCAL NATURE RESERVE

City of Wolverhampton Council
Meadow View Terrace, Wolverhampton, WV6 8NX

Smestow Valley Local Nature Reserve is a haven for wildlife, with around 125 acres of meadows, scrubland and woodland. The reserve is also close to the Staffordshire and Worcestershire Canal and Smestow Brook. Visitors can enjoy the wildlife, bird watching, flora and fauna,

Pendeford Mill Nature Reserve / ©City of Wolverhampton

Smestow Valley / ©City of Wolverhampton

cycling down the former railway track – long since removed. The route features flat and mainly level path, making it easy for walkers and cyclists. There are lots of opportunities for the keen photographer to capture rare/unusual plant specimens, alongside more commonly found favourites. Along the 2.5 mile corridor, which covers almost 120 acres, you'll find picnic areas, meadowland, woodland and the Smestow Brook which runs the length of the reserve and is part of the catchment area for the Rivers Stour and Severn. It's a great way to get across some of the city's urban sprawl without seeing a car or lorry while discovering a rich habitat for plants, birds, insects and animals.

🌐 wolverhampton.gov.uk/visiting/parks-green-spaces-and-nature-reserves

WEDNESFIELD PARK AND KING GEORGE V PLAYING FIELDS
City of Wolverhampton Council
Duke Street, Wolverhampton, WV11 1TH

Just a short walk away from Wednesfield's town centre along the Wyrley & Essington Canal you'll discover Wednesfield Park and King George V Playing Fields. It's a compact park with large playing fields alongside it – but both provide lots to do for anyone who wants to keep fit for free. Skaters and BMX bikers have their own skatepark with walls to jump and spin off, nearby is a children's play area complete with its own climbing wall. The park and fields are also home to a fitness trail, outdoor gym equipment, multi-sports court and three football pitches with changing facilities. And for those who enjoy a different pace the park has a bowling green surrounded by beautiful mature copper beech trees and traditional rose beds where you can enjoy some peace and quiet.

🌐 wolverhampton.gov.uk/visiting/parks-green-spaces-and-nature-reserves

WEST PARK

City of Wolverhampton Council
Park Road West, Wolverhampton, WV1 4PH

A fine example of a Victorian municipal park and was one of the first in the country to set a trend for the provision of areas for specific sporting activities (originally bowls, archery, and cricket). West Park is considered to be one of the best, unspoilt examples of a Victorian park left in England and is Wolverhampton's premier open space. The park features tennis courts, bowling green, tearoom and children's play area.

🌐 wolverhampton.gov.uk/visiting/parks-green-spaces-and-nature-reserves

West Park / ©City of Wolverhampton

ASHMORE PARK LIBRARY

City of Wolverhampton Council
The Hub, Griffiths Drive, Ashmore Park,
Wolverhampton, WV11 2LH

🌐 the-hub.info/library
✉ ashmorepark.library@wolverhampton.gov.uk

BILSTON LIBRARY

City of Wolverhampton Council
Mount Pleasant, Bilston, WV14 7LU

🌐 wolverhampton.gov.uk/libraries
✉ libraries@wolverhampton.gov.uk

BLAKENHALL LIBRARY

City of Wolverhampton Council
Blakenhall Community & Healthy Living Centre,
Bromley Street, WV2 3AS

🌐 wolverhampton.gov.uk/libraries
✉ libraries@wolverhampton.gov.uk

COLLINGWOOD LIBRARY

City of Wolverhampton Council
Within Broadway Gardens, Northwood Park Road,
Bushbury, WV10 8EA

🌐 wolverhampton.gov.uk/libraries
✉ libraries@wolverhampton.gov.uk

EAST PARK LIBRARY

City of Wolverhampton Council
Hurstbourne Crescent, Wolverhampton, WV1 2EE

🌐 wolverhampton.gov.uk/libraries
✉ libraries@wolverhampton.gov.uk

FINCHFIELD LIBRARY

City of Wolverhampton Council
White Oak Drive, Finchfield, WV3 9AF

🌐 wolverhampton.gov.uk/libraries
✉ libraries@wolverhampton.gov.uk

LONG KNOWLE LIBRARY

City of Wolverhampton Council
Wood End Road, Wednesfield, WV11 1YG

🌐 wolverhampton.gov.uk/libraries
✉ libraries@wolverhampton.gov.uk

LOW HILL LIBRARY

City of Wolverhampton Council
Showell Circus, Low Hill, WV10 9JL

🌐 wolverhampton.gov.uk/libraries
✉ libraries@wolverhampton.gov.uk

PENDEFORD LIBRARY

City of Wolverhampton Council
Whitburn Close, Pendeford, WV9 5NJ

🌐 wolverhampton.gov.uk/libraries
✉ libraries@wolverhampton.gov.uk

PENN LIBRARY

City of Wolverhampton Council
Coalway Avenue, Penn, WV3 7LT

🌐 wolverhampton.gov.uk/libraries
✉ libraries@wolverhampton.gov.uk

SPRING VALE LIBRARY
City of Wolverhampton Council
Bevan Avenue, Spring Vale, WV4 6SG
🌐 wolverhampton.gov.uk/libraries
✉ libraries@wolverhampton.gov.uk

WEDNESFIELD LIBRARY
City of Wolverhampton Council
2 Well Lane, Wednesfield, WV11 1XT
🌐 wolverhampton.gov.uk/libraries
✉ libraries@wolverhampton.gov.uk

TETTENHALL LIBRARY
City of Wolverhampton Council
St. Michael's Parish Centre, Upper Street,
Tettenhall, WV6 8QF
🌐 wolverhampton.gov.uk/libraries
✉ libraries@wolverhampton.gov.uk

WHITMORE REANS LIBRARY
City of Wolverhampton Council
Bargate Drive Evans Street,
Wolverhampton, WV6 0QW
🌐 wolverhampton.gov.uk/libraries
✉ libraries@wolverhampton.gov.uk

WARSTONES LIBRARY
City of Wolverhampton Council
Pinfold Grove, Penn, WV4 4PT
🌐 wolverhampton.gov.uk/libraries
✉ libraries@wolverhampton.gov.uk

WOLVERHAMPTON CENTRAL LIBRARY
City of Wolverhampton Council
Snow Hill, Wolverhampton, WV1 3AX
🌐 wolverhampton.gov.uk/libraries
✉ libraries@wolverhampton.gov.uk

INDEX

INDEX

ACKNOWLEDGEMENTS

Preliminary Research by Amy Swanson

Research and Compilation by Gemma Peters

Edited by Jenni Butterworth, Alex Nicholson-Evans & Emma Scott

Map by Tom Woolley

With thanks to teams at Birmingham City Council, Coventry City Council, Dudley Metropolitan Council, Sandwell Metropolitan Council, Solihull Metropolitan Borough Council, Walsall Council and City of Wolverhampton Council.

With thanks to the venues for providing the images and content in this guide.

The information in the book was correct at the time of publication.

Front Cover: Aston Hall Long Gallery © BMT/ Verity E. Milligan
Back Cover: Black Country Living Museum © Black Country Living Museum
               Saltwells National Nature Reserve © Martin Weaver
               Lapworth Museum of Geology © Greg Milner
               Birmingham Repertory Theatre © Ross Jukes

Supported by

PLACES I'D LIKE TO VISIT

PLACES I'D LIKE TO VISIT